Protect Wealth & Maximize Assets

Estate Planning & Trust Secrets for Suddenly Single, Widowed or Divorced

By Joe RoosEvans

CFP, CTFA, RICP, AEP, CLU, CASL, CLF, CAPP, ChFC, MBA

Contents

Dedication

This book is dedicated to my father, the person who taught me how to live life with passion, insight, and determination. And to my beautiful wife, Lori, who makes every day worth living; and to my son, Aidan, whose spirit and promise inspires me to be a better father. And finally, to every investor everywhere, no matter where you are on the road to your dreams. May you savor the joys of a rich life.

Preface

Protecting Everything You've Worked For – And Ensuring Financial Success on Your Terms

If you've worked hard all of your life to build up a nest egg - regardless of how big or small it may be - the last thing you want is for those assets to be lost unnecessarily. Losing your spouse or partner can be devastating. But it doesn't have to equate to financial hardship for you.

Even if you've received an inheritance and / or invested well over time, a large percentage of your assets could still be lost to taxes, probate, unsuitable planning, unintended beneficiaries, and / or financial predators.

The book you are holding in your hands right now will give you the knowledge you need to keep your savings, investments, property, and other assets safe - both now and in the future, for yourself, as well as for those who may be depending on you.

If your former spouse or partner was the one who always handled the financial matters in your household, fear not. This book is written in a way that you will be easily able to grasp the concepts, and to also find the resources that you need for obtaining additional guidance.

If you have found yourself "suddenly single," you are not alone. In fact, as a demographic category, single adults in the United States are growing faster than married couples – a trend that has actually continued uninterrupted since 1960.

As of 2014, there were nearly 125 million singles in the U.S., which represented more than 50% of all United States residents at that time.[1] So, whether you're widowed, divorced, or you have never been married, you're in good company.

This book was written to be your financial guide, and it will walk you through the process of planning ahead. While most people don't like to dwell on what could happen in the future, the reality is that having a viable plan in place can prevent substantial financial hardships for others in your life that you care about. This could include children and / or grandchildren, a business partner, and / or a favorite charity. Even just knowing what is available to you can be a good start.

Throughout the pages that follow, you will see various examples of people who planned ahead, as well as some who didn't. You will also learn that there are a wide variety of tools and strategies that are available to you, regardless of what your ultimate financial goals may be.

Sources

1. U.S. Singles Statistics. Single Adult Ministry.
   http://www.upcisam.com/about/singles-statistics/

About the Author

Joe RoosEvans is one of the top financial experts in the country. He started in the wealth services industry in 1982, and after several winning years, he founded Financial Resources of America (FRA). Ranked among the Top Five Percent of wealth service agencies in the world today - a leading force in the industry since 1986 - FRA is one of a group of several successful companies founded by Joe RoosEvans - all of which continue to further his reputation for leadership and innovation nationwide.

Over the years, FRA has served more than 17,000 clients who have come to Joe and his company for advice on how to best preserve their wealth. Today, the company and trust company manage over $4 billion dollars in assets.

This accomplishment is largely the net-result of Joe's passion and commitment for serving people in a quest for successful retirement lifestyles. Joe has committed his entire career to helping individuals create, grow, and protect their wealth.

All told, Joe RoosEvans is a widely recognized leader in wealth preservation, and in the financial services industry overall. An acknowledged asset-transfer specialist, radio talk show host, author, and sought-after national speaker, his professional designations include the following:

- Certified Trust and Financial Advisor (CTFA)
- Accredited Estate Planner (AEP)
- Certified Financial Planner (CFP)
- Retirement Income Certified Planner (RICP)
- Chartered Life Underwriter (CLU)
- Chartered Leadership Fellow (CLF)
- Certified Financial Planner (CFP)

- Chartered Financial Consultant (ChFC)
- Certified Wealth Preservation Planner
- Certified Asset Protection Planner
- Chartered Advisor for Senior Living (CASL)

Clients who rely on Joe RoosEvans and FRA know that they are working with well-established and experienced professionals in the wealth protection and preservation field whose sole purpose is to help them reach their goals.

Joe RoosEvans isn't your cookie-cutter financial guru. He is an innovator, educator and a passionate advocate of financial literacy, for everyone...everywhere. He is also supportive and generous, as the founder of Support Our Heroes, a charity that will benefit from every sale of this book.

His very active family includes wife, Lori, and son, Aidan, who follows in Dad's footsteps as a motorcycle racing champion. By age 10, Aidan had won 14 National titles on motorcycles, before turning to 4-wheels. At age 14 now, he has won numerous championships and rookie of the year awards in Karting, Open Wheel Micro, Midgets, and 360 Sprint Cars...and if Aidan is just getting started, Joe is running a new race to financially educate the world.

FRA

As a company that specializes in estate and income planning, FRA is committed to excellence, and the latest planning tools, so that its clients won't have to risk experimentation on their own.

For multiple generations of family members, as well as for individuals, FRA places a key focus on legacy strategies, which includes specialized trusts and long-range tax-reduction tools for beneficiaries in order to provide a plan that works in harmony with specific income and wealth preservation goals.

Along with First National Bank of Sioux Falls, the FRA family of companies has more than three decades of experience in assisting families with protecting and better controlling their wealth.

Since FRA was founded, the company has grown to become a leading authority in all aspects of income and estate planning. FRA regularly delivers high-profile seminars across the United States, where experts share their advice for maximizing the value of individuals' and families' estates in order to benefit them during their lifetime, as well as to benefit their loved ones thereafter.

FRA is able to provide income and estate planning, as well as legal and financial services, all in one complete package.

Introduction:

Protecting What You've Worked For - On Your Terms

"Planning is bringing the future into the present so that you can do something about it now."

Alan Lakein

For many of us, "saving for the future" has been a part of our regular financial lives for decades. But, while we've been taught to set money aside for emergencies, retirement, and other needs, when the time comes to transfer those assets to the next generation, a favorite charity, and / or others who are near and dear to you, countless funds can be unnecessarily diverted into the hands of creditors, predators, in-laws, out-laws, and / or Uncle Sam.

Although many might feel that "death and taxes" are inevitable in the road of life, the truth is that with the right estate plan in place, you can have much more control over who inherits what, while at the same time keeping more - in some cases, much more - intact for your needs, as well as for those you love and care about.

Financial, Income and Estate Planning Are Not "Do It Yourself" Projects

Most of us don't like to dwell on getting older - especially if it entails having to think about what will happen when we are gone. That's why the majority of people put off and procrastinate - oftentimes until it's much too late to do anything about it.

Unfortunately, this can end up costing others - particularly those such as a business partner, a special needs child, or even a favorite charity that could have benefitted from your generosity. With that in mind, burying our heads in the sand is simply not a stable strategy for preparing for the inevitable.

But creating a customized estate plan is.

In doing so, while many people may gather bits and pieces of information via the Internet or from financial magazines, the reality is that moving forward with just some of the details - especially if they don't pertain to you and your situation - can actually do much more harm than good.

For example, did you know that it is unlikely that all of your assets will be passed on as you specified in your last will and testament? Likewise, putting assets such as your home or a bank account in the name of an adult child can also have some serious adverse consequences.

And, what about a child or other loved one who may have special needs? According to the National Organization on Disability, nearly one in five Americans has a physical, sensory, or intellectual disability. If you are part of such a family, would your loved one be assured of the proper care - and the funding for it - if something were to happen to you?

When it comes to constructing a viable estate plan that is specific to your and your loved ones' unique needs, unless you are well-versed in this particular area of wealth planning, it is essential to work with qualified professionals who can guide you in the right direction. They can also help you to ensure that the plan you create today will "roll with the changes" over time as your life and your circumstances change.

As someone who is (suddenly) single – whether that be due to divorce, the death of a spouse, or never having been married – you face some real challenges as it pertains to keeping your hard-earned savings and investments, well – safe.

In moving forward, then, it is vitally important to be familiar with the tools and strategies that may be available to you. That is exactly what this book will provide. So, are you ready to learn the secrets about how you can take control of your situation, both now and far into the future?

Let's turn the page and let's begin.

Today is a great day to get started NOW!

Chapter 1:

The "Problem" with Successful Saving and Investing

What You Don't Know Can Hurt Those You Love

"All progress takes place outside the comfort zone."

Michael John Boba

Let me tell you about a great guy named Richard (not his real name, in order to protect his privacy) and his situation - a situation that could happen to you or to anyone if proper estate planning is not done.

Throughout his entire life, Richard was considered a go-getter when it came to making and investing money. This started at a young age when he began his newspaper route and opened his first savings account.

When Richard was just 12 years old, he asked his father if he could open an investment account and start trading stocks. In doing so, Richard learned how to analyze companies based on their earnings and track record and invest accordingly. Due to his investment savvy, Richard had accumulated more than $20,000 by the time he started high school.

It was no surprise, then, that Richard started his own manufacturing company as soon as he graduated from college. Although he kept the company small in terms of overhead and number of employees, Richard did business with clients all over the world. And the money just kept pouring in.

Yet, based on his extremely busy schedule, Richard never found the time to sit down and plan ahead for what would happen with his company - or his family - if he died suddenly or became incapacitated. And that decision to do nothing would later prove to be detrimental.

One night, while driving home from his company's Christmas party, Richard was involved in a head-on collision, killing him instantly. He was just 61 years old.

For the next several months, Richard's three adult children (who Richard had with his ex-wife) had to endure the lengthy process of probate. At the same time, because Richard had no business succession plan in place, there was no real direction in terms of how the company would move forward without him.

One by one, clients began to take their business elsewhere. Seeing the writing on the wall, the company's employees also moved on, eventually bankrupting the business. When it was all said and done, due to taxes and probate fees, Richard's children received less than half the value of his estate. To make matters worse, because Richard had never changed the beneficiary designation on a long-held life insurance policy, his ex-wife received a benefit payout of $500,000.

The Consequences of Not Having an Estate Plan

Even if you've been a good saver and investor all of your life, what ends up happening with your hard-earned assets will depend primarily on how - and how well - you plan ahead. If you've accumulated a nice nest egg and / or built a business from the ground up, not planning for what could be ahead can have detrimental consequences to a long list of loved ones and associates...including yourself.

Most people have three primary phases of their estate. These include the:

- Accumulation Phase
- Distribution Phase
- Transfer Phase

The accumulation phase consists of saving, investing, and building up assets, primarily during the working, or earning, years. Here we can typically afford to take on more risk in return for the opportunity to attain more growth.

Next, the distribution phase starts when we enter into retirement. This is when we bring in the proverbial "harvest," or the fruits of our labor from our saving and investing over time. It is also when we convert some (or all) of what we have saved into a retirement income stream with the goal of sustaining that income for as long as we need it.

The third phase, transfer, begins when an individual (or their spouse) passes away. In order to prepare for this phase, many people will create a will and / or set up various trusts in order to help with passing on their property and assets to those they leave behind.

Unfortunately, many people will oftentimes only concentrate on the first two phases, without giving much thought to the third. This could be because they believe they have more time to take care of it, and / or because most of us don't enjoy thinking about what will happen when we are gone.

But not considering the transfer phase could leave your loved ones in a big financial bind - one that could have been prevented with some advance estate planning. So, it is important to keep in mind that, just because you're doing a good job of saving, planning for retirement, and / or managing money, doesn't mean that you're doing good estate planning - which is *true* wealth planning. This requires addressing all of the key areas, not just some of them.

So, what exactly can happen if you don't have an estate plan?

For starters, even if you don't have an actual plan in place, your property and assets will still be transferred to somebody...but it's highly likely that it won't be to the individual (or individuals) that you intended, nor will it be in the manner that you may have wished.

Many people are under the impression that financial planning and estate planning are all one in the same. But this is not the case at all. For example, with financial planning, your current and future financial state is evaluated in order to predict future income, asset values, and a viable income withdrawal plan for the future when you retire.

Estate planning, on the other hand, focuses more on preparing for the transfer of your assets and property after you are gone. It also deals with pre-planning for other potential situations such as disability and incapacity. But combining financial and estate planning, you engage in true wealth planning.

Estate planning doesn't only pertain to what happens upon a person's death, either. In addition, this type of planning can also entail making arrangements for the management of your assets if you should become mentally or physically able to do so yourself.

Even if you don't feel like you are wealthy, you still need an estate plan in order to help ensure that what you have built up is properly protected for those you love - and from creditors, predators, and Uncle Sam. Without a plan, a large chunk of any sized estate could be eaten up by these entities, leaving little - if anything - for your family.

If, for instance, you don't have a will in place, state law will determine who inherits your assets, as well as who will be in charge of settling your estate. In addition, if you have young children who are still minors, and you don't have a plan in place that names specific guardians for them, the court will make that decision for you. This alone can be life-altering for those who are left behind and whom you love. It could also mean that those whom you don't love could end up with a portion of your estate.

Even if you are currently in good health, the chances of becoming disabled at some point in your lifetime may be higher than you think. According to the United States Social Security Administration, someone who is just 20 years old has a one in four chance of contracting a disabling condition between now and the time they retire. And, based on U.S. Census Bureau statistics, of those who become disabled, there is a 38% chance that the disability would last for five years or longer!

With all this in mind, estate planning is truly important, as it embraces your overall financial and wealth preservation situation - putting everything together in one convenient "package" that provides direction for your wishes, along with the tools for doing so.

In the absence of any estate planning, you and your loved ones will likely be required to go through time-consuming and costly legal processes, such as establishing a guardianship. A good, solid estate plan will also include direction regarding your medical care, such as whether or not you want to receive life-saving measures, if you are not able to make such decisions on your own.

Unfortunately, when individuals don't make their wishes known in advance, the situation can put loved ones in an even more difficult situation during an already tough time. Given all of this, most people would agree that having a good, solid estate plan in place is preferable to leaving your medical and financial circumstances to chance.

Chapter 1 Quiz

At the end of each chapter, there will be a short five-question quiz. These questions will help you to determine how much of the information you have retained. The answers can be found immediately after the questions in each chapter.

1. Which of the below describe the three primary phases of one's estate?

a. Accumulation; Distribution; Transfer

b. Transfer; Saving; Investing

c. Saving; Investing; Allocation

d. None of the Above

2. Estate planning pertains to which of the following?

a. What happens upon a person's death

b. Making arrangements for the management of assets if one becomes incapacitated

c. Both a and b

d. Neither a or b

3. True or False: In the absence of any estate planning, you and your loved ones will likely be required to go through time-consuming and legal processes, such as establishing a guardianship.

4. If you do not have a will in place, state law will determine which of the following?

a. Who inherits your assets

b. Who will be in charge of settling your estate

c. Both a and b

d. Neither a or b

5. The _____ phase of your estate starts when you enter into retirement.

a. transfer

b. saving

c. distribution

d. None of the Above

Chapter 1 Quiz Answers

1. a

2. c

3. True

4. c

5. c

Chapter 2:

Top Estate Planning Mistakes and How to Avoid Them

Common Estate Planning Mistakes that Could Cost You

"Successful people keep moving. They make mistakes; but they don't quit."

Conrad Hilton

Regardless of your age or taste in movies, it is likely that you are familiar with the late Hollywood star James Dean. Unfortunately, at the height of his career, Dean was killed in an auto accident at the age of only 24.

Yet, while he was quite a young man, due to his "heart throb" persona, Dean was a very wealthy man at the time of his passing. Unfortunately, he died without having a will - and because of that, under the law of intestate succession, his estranged father ended up inheriting all of Dean's assets, even though he had abandoned James when he was just nine years old.

Due to his lack of planning, rather than millions of dollars going to the people that James Dean loved and cared about, all of his money instead went to his biological father, who Dean never really even knew.

As you can see, financial matters - even of great proportion - can go south, if they are not properly planned for. One "unintended beneficiary" can be Uncle Sam - primarily in the form of transfer and estate taxes. While you may be somewhat familiar with federal estate taxes, it is important to also be mindful of how your individual state factors in.

That is because there are some states throughout the country that differ somewhat in the amount of their estate tax exemption, as well as in terms of additional taxes such as a state tax. Therefore, working with a professional who is familiar with estate transfer, as well as both federal and state estate taxes is essential.

Common Estate Planning Mistakes that Could Cost You

Although many people state that they should create an estate plan for the purpose of avoiding probate, recent statistics show that the majority of Americans don't plan because they lack awareness as to why they should[1] - and due in part to this lack of awareness also comes a number of myths and misconceptions.

Unfortunately, even though you may take some steps towards creating an estate plan, because it can be such a complex and individualized process, it can be very easy to make mistakes. Even just one small mistake could be extremely costly and detrimental to the entire plan.

Here are the top ten estate planning mistakes that are most often made, starting with #10:

#10: Letting Your Loved Ones Go to Probate Court

One of the biggest mistakes that people can make is allowing their estate to go to probate. Although most people have heard the term "probate," many are not familiar with what the process entails, as well as just how costly going through probate can be for your loved ones and survivors.

What exactly is probate?

Probate is defined as the legal proceeding in which a deceased person's will is submitted to a court - which is often referred to as the probate court - that has legal authority over the settlement of the estate.

During the probate process, the court will determine whether or not the individual's will is valid. In addition, an executor of the estate is appointed. (The executor may also be referred to as the personal representative). Once an executor has been appointed, they will carry out the terms of the will.

The probate process can be lengthy, as well as costly - the expenses of which come directly out of the estate's assets, in turn, lessening what your heirs will receive. And, if there are debts to be paid, it is possible that your loved ones may not receive anything at all.

Also, anyone with a possible claim can contest the will, such as in-laws, outlaws, creditors, and predators – and in turn, cost loved ones dearly. (And yes, even if you are widowed or divorced, it is possible that your former in-laws could have claim to some or all of your assets).

#9: Believing All Living Trust Plans are the Same

Another key estate planning mistake is the belief that all living trust plans are the same. Just like in any other area of financial planning, there is no one-size-fits-all tool that meets every need across the board. Knowing what living trust options are available - and which will or won't serve you the best - is essential.

In its most basic sense, a trust is a legal device for the management of property. Through a trust, one person (the "grantor") transfers the legal title to property to another person (the "trustee"), who will then manage the property in a specified manner for the benefit of a third person (the "beneficiary").

In other words, the legal rights of property ownership and control rest with the trustee, who then has the responsibility of managing the property as directed by the grantor in a trust document for the ultimate benefit of the trust beneficiary.

A "living trust" takes effect during the lifetime of the grantor, whereas a "testamentary trust" is created by a will and does not go into effect until you pass away. (The different types of trusts will be discussed in further detail later in the book).

#8: Failing to Address What Will Happen If You Become Disabled

While it is important to have a plan in place for what happens with property and assets after a person dies, there can also be a number of serious consequences if an illness or injury renders you physically and / or mentally disabled and unable to make financial and medical decisions on your own.

Although each state has its own definition of incapacity, in general, someone who is incapacitated is impaired to the point of being incapable of making or communicating responsible decisions concerning themselves or their property.

If you should become incapacitated, a legal guardianship proceeding may be required. This entails a court proceeding in which a judge does the following:

- Determines whether or not you are actually, legally incapacitated, and
- Appoints a guardian (also known as a conservator) who will handle your affairs, if necessary.

In this case, the judge can appoint a guardian who will make all of your personal decisions - including where you will live, and / or a guardian who will handle all of your assets. To make matters worse, this lengthy, complicated process can be expensive...and public! For example, in order to represent you, the prospective guardian may first need to hire an attorney. And, the court may also appoint another attorney, who is oftentimes referred to as a guardian ad litem, in order to represent you.

#7: Not Protecting Your Beneficiaries from Themselves

If you have an adult child or other relative who may not have the best of money management skills, it could be that if he or she inherits a large sum of money, they will spend it all within a short period of time.

The right estate plan, however, could include tools and strategies - such as only releasing a certain amount of money throughout a set time period - that can help to protect a beneficiary who is a spendthrift from blowing all of their inheritance at once.

#6: Not Protecting Your Beneficiaries from Third Parties

In addition to protecting beneficiaries from themselves, there could also be third parties out there, such as creditors or even unscrupulous individuals, who will try to come after money in the estate - especially if the estate is going through the probate process and information about assets and property becomes public knowledge.

Having the right estate plan in place can keep this from happening. It can also keep your very private financial details out of the public limelight.

#5: Thinking Your Living Trust Covers Your IRA or Other Retirement Accounts

For many people, it is a given that their largest asset is the money that they've saved in an IRA and / or employer-sponsored retirement account like a 401(k). But what isn't so widely known is that money in these types of accounts is not typically covered in a will.

Rather, inheritance from IRAs and retirement plans is generally doled out according to beneficiary designation forms that are filled out by the account holder. This is the case, regardless of what is stated in one's will.

In other words, beneficiary designation overrides what is written in wills. However, a living trust will not offer asset protection while the trustor is still alive. So, assuming that this is the case could be costly to yourself, and possibly to your loved ones.

After the trustor passes away, though, beneficiaries can "stretch out" IRA payouts. Likewise, a special type of trust that is referred to as an IRA Beneficiary Trust, can protect inherited retirement account balances from creditors (including those involved in a person's bankruptcy), divorce decree requirements, and even from certain long-term care expenses.

Without such a trust, inherited IRA and other retirement plan funds could be at substantial risk. As an example, based on the *Clark v. Rameker* case that went all the way to the U.S. Supreme Court, the Court held - in a unanimous decision - that "inherited IRAs are not exempt from the beneficiary's creditors because inherited IRAs are no 'retirement funds' within the meaning of 11 USC 522(b)(3)(C) of the federal Bankruptcy Code." As a result, the creditors of the beneficiary of an inherited IRA may attach the inherited IRA.[2] (We will discuss more on IRA Beneficiary Trusts later in this book).

#4: Thinking Your Living Trust is Enough

While having a living trust can be beneficial to your overall estate plan, some people make the mistake of assuming that once they have established such a vehicle, that is all they need. This, however, is not the case.

A living trust is set up during an individual's life. As the owner of a living trust, you can be both the grantor and the trustee. But just simply setting up a living trust is not enough. You also need to fund your living trust, meaning that you transfer legal title to property to the trustee.

In fact, it is essential to clearly distinguish the concept of just merely creating a living trust, from the concept of actually funding it. Here, for instance, even though you may have created such a trust, it is not funded until you have transferred property to it. In other words, the trust is only considered to be funded when the trustee legally owns some property - which is known as the "trust property."

#3: Believing the Person(s) Who You Name to Act as Trustee Will Know What to Do

A trustee is the person who is essentially "trusted" to safeguard and invest the trust property, pay the legitimate debts, expenses, and taxes of the trust, and to distribute the remaining property in accordance with the terms of the trust document.

This can be a big job, so it is important to ensure that the individual you have named to act as the trustee will know what to do. Unfortunately, this is not necessarily always the case. In addition to having to use their discretion with regard to what happens with the trust's assets, the job of a trustee can go on for many years.

Many people simply assume that a family member or other loved one is up for the task. This, however, can be dangerous, costly, and in some cases, extremely detrimental to your loved ones and survivors.

#2: Not Keeping Up with Changes

Because our lives are a series of constant changes, no financial or estate plan is ever really "complete." With that in mind, your estate plan needs to keep up with the changes in your life, as well as with other changes that are out of your control, such as new or updated tax laws.

Just think back over the past ten years of your life. Have you experienced a birth or death in the family, marriage or divorce, a new job or business, a move to a new home, or all of the above? If so, it could have a major impact on your plan.

By not keeping up with such changes, you may find that an ex-spouse ends up inheriting money from your life insurance policy, a deceased spouse is still named as the beneficiary on your retirement plan, one of your grandchildren is unintentionally left out of your will, and / or a whole host of other not-so-pleasant scenarios that could substantially cost your loved ones financially, as well as emotionally.

#1: Procrastinating

The number one estate planning myth is that, because people think they're "too busy" to move forward, "too young" to worry about it, "not wealthy enough" to have an issue, or already "protected" because their family will take care of them, they procrastinate...which makes it highly likely that when something happens, it will be much too late.

Based on recent statistics, up to approximately 68% of pre-retirees today have no or inadequate estate or retirement planning. If you want to ensure that you're in the 32% that *are* protected with a plan, then it is important that you take the necessary steps to create a plan that works for you and your loved ones.[2]

Taking a Closer Look at Estate Taxes and Proper Estate Tax Planning

Estate planning for single individuals can be somewhat challenging. There are a lot of decisions that must be made. While it can be tempting to ignore this type of planning, knowing that you have a plan in place can reduce stress, as well as anxiety on survivors.

When a person dies without a will, their assets will be distributed according to the applicable intestate succession laws in their state, as well as rules that have to do with their marital status. For example, for single individuals, his or her surviving parents and siblings will inherit equal shares of their estate.

If, however, one of their parents is deceased, the surviving parent will inherit both shares. Likewise, if a sibling died and is survived by his or her own descendants, those descendants will inherit that share. If there are no surviving first-degree (immediate) relatives, the estate will be divided equally between remaining family members. And, if there are no surviving relatives, the state will receive the assets.

States with an Estate or Inheritance Tax

Does Your State Have An Estate or Inheritance Tax?

State Estate & Inheritance Tax Rates & Exemptions in 2017

VT
$2.75M
16%

NH

MA
$1M
0.8%-16%

RI
$1.515M
0.8%-16%

CT
$2M
7.2%-12%

NJ
Estate: $2M
0.8%-16%
Inheritance: 0%-16%

DE
$5.49M
0.8%-16%

MD
Estate: $3M
16%
Inheritance: 0%-10%

DC
$2M
8%-16%

HI
$5.49M
10%-15.7%

Note: Exemption amounts are shown for state estate taxes only.
Inheritance taxes are levied on the posthumous transfer of assets based
on the relationship to the decendent; different rates and exemptions
apply depending on the relationship.
Source: Family Business Coalition; state statutes.

State Has an Estate Tax

State Has an Inheritance Tax

III State Has Both an Estate
& Inheritance Tax

Source: Tax Foundation

For updated figures and additional details regarding individual states' estate tax figures,
go to: http://faturl.com/90v4km1/?selected=0

Don't Put Off What Could Be the Most Important Plan You Ever Make

If you haven't started creating your wealth plan, don't feel alone, as you actually fall into
the majority. However, this is one area where you don't want to be "average," because
it could cost those you care about significantly.

The first step to getting started is to make a call to a professional - now. The first step to getting started is to make a call to a professional - now. Even if you already have a plan in place, it could warrant a review. Contact us at FRA Trust at (800) 279-9785, or at http://fratrust.com/contact-us/ for a no cost, no obligation review.

If you have people, causes, and / or other entities in your life that you love, having a viable estate plan in place can provide them with benefits for many years in the future. And, they will always remember you for it. (The same doesn't hold true if the bulk of your assets end up with creditors, predators, or Uncle Sam as your biggest beneficiary!)

It is important that you start getting your wealth planning in place today. Don't put it off. Our three-step, 21-day process is much easier and faster than you may think. There are no surprises, and you'll be glad you did.

Chapter 2 Sources

1. Top 10 Estate Planning Mistakes. FRA Trust.

2. Supreme Court Decision on Inherited IRAs May Change Calculus on Structuring Beneficiary Designations. (https://www.bna.com/supreme-court-decisions-n17179893782/)

Chapter 2 Quiz

These questions are here to help you with determining how much of the chapter information you have retained. The answers can be found following the last quiz question in each of the chapters.

1. _____ is defined as the legal proceeding in which a deceased person's will is submitted to a court that has legal authority over the settlement of the estate.

a. estate planning

b. probate

c. intestate

d. None of the Above

2 In its most basic sense, a(n) _____ is a legal device for the management of property.

a. estate plan

b. trust

c. executor

d. beneficiary

3. During the probate process, which of the following takes place?

a. The court will determine whether or not the will is valid

b. An executor of the estate is appointed

c. Both a and b

d. Neither a or b

4. A(n) _____ takes effect during the lifetime of the grantor, whereas a(n) _____ is created by a will and does not go into effect until one passes away.

a. ILIT / CRT

b. testamentary trust / living trust

c. living trust / testamentary trust

d. CRAT / CRUT

5. True or False: Once you have established a living trust, this is really all you need in order to have a complete estate plan.

Chapter 2 Quiz Answers

1. b

2. b

3. c

4. c

5. False

Chapter 3:

You Don't Need to Be Rich to Have an Estate

What Your Estate Is...and Isn't

"It's not how much money you make but how much money you keep, how hard it works for you, and how many generations you keep it for."

Robert Kiyosaki

While discussions about estate planning often focus on married couples, estate planning for a single person is equally as important. In many instances, a single individual may need to do things differently. And, just like with married couples, the consequences of not having a well-coordinated estate plan can create some significant problems.

Most single individuals own assets in their names individually, and may also own some assets as a joint tenant with right of survivorship. Other assets, such as life insurance or retirement assets, will be distributed at the individual's passing according to the terms of their beneficiary designation.

How these varying assets are titled and how the beneficiary designations are prepared will directly impact who will get control of the assets, as well as how they will be distributed at the person's death.

Without the right plan, things could turn out vastly different than intended when it comes to planning ahead. For instance, as an investigative journalist, Allen once spent several months working on a series of articles about what happens to the estates of people who die without a will.

In short, it can be ugly.

In one case that Allen investigated, he found that a surrogate court judge had appointed three lawyers as "guardians" of potential heirs to the estate of a never-married, childless woman. Ostensibly in search of heirs, these lawyers spent part of the deceased woman's estate on a junket to Puerto Rico for themselves!

In the end, one of the lawyers had siphoned off more than $116,000 in fees, while the deceased woman's 14 cousins only received inheritances of $33,150 each.

What Your Estate Is...And Isn't

Throughout life, many of us have the goal of "building up." We work hard to build our career, build up our asset base, and build up our net worth over time. Many people may also work to build up and grow their own business. So, it may seem counterintuitive then that the primary function of a good estate plan is to properly safeguard one's wealth. But it is - at least in a manner of speaking.

In its most basic sense, a taxable estate is "the portion of a person's net assets that are taxable upon his or her death". With that in mind, a taxable estate is defined as the total value of a deceased person's assets that are subject to taxation, minus liabilities, and minus the prescribed tax-deductible portion of assets that are left behind by the deceased.[1]

In most cases, a person's taxable estate will likely consist of some or all of the following types of assets:

- Cash
- CD's
- Stocks, bonds, and mutual funds (including retirement accounts such as IRAs and 401k's)
- Real estate
- Personal property
- Life insurance
- Business(es) owned
- Autos and other vehicles
- Jewelry

There will also typically be at least some amount of liabilities. These may include:

- Mortgage balance
- Home equity loan balance
- Auto loan(s)
- Student loan(s)
- Other loan(s)
- Credit card balance(s)

After death, it is possible that your assets and property may be subject to estate taxes, based on the total value of the estate. This is determined by adding up the total amount of the estate's assets and then subtracting the total amount of the estate's liabilities.

The following items are also allowed to be deducted in order to determine the taxable portion of an estate:

- Funeral expenses that are paid out of the estate
- Debts that are owed by the decedent at the time of his or her death
- Value of the assets passed on to the decedent's spouse[2]

For a full, updated list of items, go to: https://form.jotform.com/80246770199161

There are a number of strategies that can be used to help in reducing - or eliminating altogether - the estate taxes that are due. These techniques and strategies will be discussed throughout this book.

Determining Your Estate's Overall Value

In getting started with your estate plan, a good first step is to take an inventory of your assets, and then to estimate their value. It is also a good idea to consider potential beneficiaries, as well as those you would consider as trusted individuals to serve in the roles of a potential guardian for minor children (if applicable) and / or powers of attorney.

Creating your estate plan will begin with determining what exactly constitutes your taxable estate. This means making a determination of what you have "built up" over the years, and then determining where you may be taxed, how those taxes can be eliminated or reduced, and to whom those assets will go when you are no longer here (or possibly even prior to that time in certain cases).

Detailed Asset Worksheet

Primary Residence	
Address	
Assessed Value	
Name on the Deed	
Mortgage Loan Balance	
Mortgage Terms	
Mortgage Lender(s)	
Secondary Residence	
Address	
Assessed Value	
Name on the Deed	
Mortgage Loan Balance	
Mortgage Terms	
Lender(s)	
Rental Income	

Secondary Residence #2	
Address	
Assessed Value	
Name on the Deed	
Mortgage Loan Balance	
Mortgage Terms	
Lender(s)	
Rental Income	
Undeveloped Land	
Address	
Assessed Value	
Name on the Deed	
Mortgage Loan Balance	
Mortgage Terms	
Lender(s)	
Co-Signed Mortgage	
Address	
Assessed Value	
Name on the Deed	
Mortgage Loan Balance	
Mortgage Terms	
Lender(s)	
Primary Vehicles	
Vehicle Year, Make and Model	
Assessed Value	
Title Holder	
Amount Remaining on Loan	
Loan Term	
Lender	
Secondary Vehicle(s)	
Vehicle Year, Make and Model	
Assessed Value	
Title Holder	
Amount Remaining on Loan	
Loan Term	
Lender	
Other Assets	
Item Depreciation	
Value	
Item Depreciation	
Value	
Item Depreciation	

Value	
Item Depreciation	
Value	
Item Depreciation	
Value	
Item Depreciation	
Value	
Loan	
Loan Description	
Name on the Loan	
Amount Remaining on the Loan	
Loan Terms	
Lender	
Loan #2	
Loan Description	
Name on the Loan	
Amount Remaining on the Loan	
Loan Terms	
Lender	
Loan #3	
Loan Description	
Name on the Loan	
Amount Remaining on the Loan	
Loan Terms	
Lender	
Property Insurance Primary Residence	
Address	
Policy Number	
Premium	
Terms	
Institution	
Property Insurance Secondary Residence	
Address	
Policy Number	
Premium	
Terms	
Institution	
Property Insurance Secondary Residence #2	
Address	
Policy Number	
Premium	

Terms	
Institution	
Primary Vehicle Insurance	
Primary Vehicle	
Policy Number	
Premium	
Terms	
Institution	
Secondary Vehicle Insurance	
Primary Vehicle	
Policy Number	
Premium	
Terms	
Institution	
Personal Insurance - Life	
Policy Number	
Premium	
Terms	
Institution	
Beneficiary	
Personal Insurance - Health	
Policy Number	
Premium	
Terms	
Institution	
Beneficiary	
Personal Insurance - Long-Term Care	
Policy Number	
Premium	
Terms	
Institution	
Beneficiary	
Personal Insurance - Umbrella Liability	
Policy Number	
Premium	
Terms	
Institution	
Beneficiary	
Personal Insurance - Other	
Policy Number	
Premium	
Terms	

Institution	
Beneficiary	
Personal Insurance - Other	
Policy Number	
Premium	
Terms	
Institution	
Beneficiary	
Personal Insurance - Other	
Policy Number	
Premium	
Terms	
Institution	
Beneficiary	
Stock Market Holdings	
Details	
Current Value	
Broker/Manager Contact Info.	
Stock Market Holdings	
Details	
Current Value	
Broker/Manager Contact Info	
Stock Market Holdings	
Details	
Current Value	
Broker/Manager Contact Info	
Bond	
Details	
Current Value	
Maturation Date	
Institution	
Bond	
Details	
Current Value	
Maturation Date	
Institution	
CD	
Details	
Current Value	
Maturation Date	
Institution	
CD	

Details	
Current Value	
Maturation Date	
Institution	
Public Pension	
Details	
Estimated Payments	
Private Pension	
Details	
Estimated Payments	
Mutual Funds	
Details	
Current Value	
Institution	
Cash and Cash Equivalents	
Details	
Value	

To download additional copies of these forms, go to:
http://www.frafinancial.com/what-we-do/heres-to-the-good-life.php

Once you have outlined everything you own and everything you owe, it is possible to move forward with determining your net worth. Doing so entails adding up all of your assets, and then subtracting the total amount of your liabilities. The resulting figure is your overall net worth.

Net Worth Worksheet

Assets		Liabilities	
Cash and Cash Equiv.	*Total*	*Mortgage (principal)*	$
Cash	$		
Checking / Savings	$	*Other Debt*	*Total*
Other	$	Home Improvement Loan(s)	$
		Student Loan(s)	$
Real Property (Market Value)	*Total*	Credit Card(s)	$

Real Estate	$	Car Loan(s)	$
Car	$	Other	$
Personal Property	$		
Other	$	Taxes Owed	Total
		State and Local	$
Investments	Total	Federal	$
CDs	$		
Stocks / Bonds	$	Contractual Obligations	Total
Mutual Funds	$	Lease(s), tuition, etc.	$
Other	$	Other	$
Retirement Accounts	Total	Total Liabilities	$
IRA			
Pension Fund (vested)		Total Assets	$
Other		Minus (-)	
		Liabilities	$
Other	$	Equals (=)	
Total Assets	$	**Net Worth**	$

To download these forms, go to: http://www.frafinancial.com/what-we-do/heres-to-the-good-life.php

Now that you have a better idea of your net worth, it's time to determine how to protect it, and how to best transfer it with the least amount of risk. For many people, saving and investing has been a key part of their planning process for the future. But oftentimes it just takes one unexpected event such as death or disability to unravel all that a person has worked for over many years.

Having an estate plan will possibly allow you to not only protect assets from taxes and creditors, but it will also provide you with control over who receives what - and who doesn't. While having a will is certainly a key part of an estate plan, having *only* a will is far from enough.

Why Just a Simple Will Is Not an Estate Plan

When someone dies without having a valid will, they are said to have died intestate. When this occurs, the resulting probate proceeding is oftentimes referred to as an "intestacy proceeding." This is because the state laws of intestate succession - also known as laws of descent and distribution - will typically be applied to any asset or property that is owned by the decedent at death that is not held in a will substitute form.

Wills are defined as being a legally enforceable declaration of how an individual wants his or her assets to be distributed upon their death. Within a will, an individual may also state whom they wish to act as the guardian for their minor children. Without a will, the distribution of a person's property and assets are left up to the government. In some cases, assets could even end up becoming property of the state.

Many people feel that if they have a written will in place, they have adequately prepared themselves and their survivors for the inevitable. Unfortunately, this is far from being the case - and, while having a will is certainly an essential part of the overall estate planning process, it is really just one small piece of the complete puzzle.

One of the primary components of estate planning involves the use of trusts. Without knowing what a trust is and how it works, though, it is difficult to know if this is something that you really need.

In many cases, a trust can be a crucial part of your estate plan. Perhaps the most important reason to have a trust is to protect the financial interests of your family. Trusts can also allow you to be more selective about the distribution of your assets following your passing. These instruments can be particularly useful if you are leaving money to minors.

There are a variety of reasons to use trusts in estate planning. First, in many ways, a trust can be considered as the "manifesto" for the distribution, safeguarding, and control of your assets in the event of your incapacity or passing away. When you elect a trustee, you provide the trustee with the authority to act as your "agent" in order to ensure that your wishes will be carried out the way that you want them to be.

Contrary to popular belief, you don't have to be hugely wealthy in order to use a trust. These instruments are enormously useful estate planning tools for lots of people, and they can help your money to stretch further when you are gone - provided that you get the right estate planning advice.

Nearly all modern estate plans incorporate at least one type of trust. Some trusts are used in an attempt to either postpone, reduce, or even to eliminate estate taxes. Other types of trusts can be used for dealing with particular issues such as a special needs child or a second marriage.

Trust documents can typically provide you with a great deal of freedom. Therefore, you can be fairly specific, as well as creative - depending on what you are trying to accomplish - when you are setting up your trust.

Trusts are typically composed of four key components. These include the following:

- **Grantor** - The grantor is the individual who sets up the trust.
- **Trustee and Successor Trustee** - This is the person(s) or the entity that will follow your wishes as per the trust document and that will manage the trust following your passing.
- **Beneficiary (or Beneficiaries)** - These are the individuals or entities that will benefit from the trust's assets.
- **Property / Assets** - There is also property and / or assets that are placed inside of the trust. These properties and / or assets are the items such as money and investments, or physical property like real estate, that will actually make up the trust.

As with any type of financial planning, there is never a "one size fits all" solution when it comes to estate planning. And, while a trust can be flexible, these vehicles are also quite complex to set up. Working with an expert estate planning team, then, is peace of mind that your plan is specific to your unique needs.

Understanding Revocable versus Irrevocable Trusts

There are two fundamental types of trusts. These are testamentary and living trusts. A trust that is set up to be established and operated after a person's death is known as a testamentary trust. A living trust - which is also known as "inter vivos" - is set up during a person's lifetime.

Living trusts are termed either as revocable or irrevocable, according to the following definitions:

- A revocable trust allows you to retain full control of all your assets in the trust, with complete freedom to change or revoke the terms and conditions of your trust at any time.
- An irrevocable trust does not give you full control of any assets held in it, and you are not allowed to make changes to this type of trust without the consent of the beneficiaries. The upside to an irrevocable trust, however, is that it is not subject to estate taxes. That is because, by placing assets into an irrevocable trust, it essentially removes ownership - and in turn, tax responsibility, from you / your estate, provided that a proper amount of time has elapsed.

With a revocable trust, if the trust owner has any type of second thoughts about the trust provisions, the terms of the trust can be modified - or the trust can be changed or even revoked altogether.

The downside to a revocable trust is that the assets that are in the trust are still considered to be the trust owner's personal assets for both creditor and estate tax purposes - and because of this, they will be included in his or her estate for estate tax purposes. (It also means that if the individual is sued, the assets could be at risk).

In some cases, a revocable living trust may be used as a partial substitute for a will - although typically a will is still needed in order to cover any of the assets that were not transferred into the trust.

These types of trusts are a very common planning tool for avoiding probate, because the property and assets that are held inside of the trust will pass directly to the trust beneficiary (or beneficiaries) upon the trust maker's death.

Many people will name themselves as the trustee of a revocable trust, thus being able to stay in control of the trust's assets during their lifetime. Then, with this type of a trust, the successor trustee (the individual who is appointed to handle the trust following the trust maker's passing) will simply transfer the ownership to the named trust beneficiaries.

A revocable living trust can be altered at any point during the trust maker's lifetime. This means that beneficiary designations may be changed, income may be received or altered, and / or the trust can be discontinued altogether if the individual so chooses. In addition, the trust maker has full access to the trust's principal. The terms of the trust will then become irrevocable after the trust maker dies.

Because of this full discretion and control, however, the assets - and their value - will continue to remain a part of the trust maker's estate. This means that they will typically be included in the trust maker's taxable estate when accounting for estate taxes.

There are certain provisions that can be included in a revocable living trust, though, that can help to reduce the individual's estate tax liability. For example, certain types of continuing trusts could be set up for managing the assets going forward.

On the other hand, an irrevocable trust is a type of trust that usually cannot be changed once the agreement has been signed. Irrevocable trusts are used a great deal in estate planning because they can essentially remove the value of property from a person's estate so that the assets cannot be taxed when the individual passes away.

This occurs because, when the person who transfers his or her assets into an irrevocable trust and gives assets to the trust, the individual will no longer own those assets - and in turn, these assets cannot be taxed to his or her estate.

Irrevocable trusts are also used for asset protection in a similar manner. This is because when assets are placed into the trust and essentially removed from the person's estate, they cannot be obtained by creditors.

Understanding Life Insurance Trusts

If a life insurance policy is owned by an individual, then the death benefit proceeds from the policy will be included in his or her taxable estate. This means that the dollar amount of the death benefits could also be subject to estate tax - and in turn, increasing the amount of estate taxes that are due. Using an irrevocable trust can change this, though.

For example, for those who are trying to reduce the amount of their taxable estate and / or trying to figure out how to eliminate estate taxes, there is a way to use life insurance - but it isn't by owning it in your own name.

In this case, an irrevocable life insurance trust, or ILIT, can be created for the purpose of either purchasing a new life insurance policy or for holding and owning an existing one. Here, then, the ILIT actually becomes the owner of the life insurance policy.

Because of this, the death benefit proceeds will technically be held outside of the insured's taxable estate - therefore reducing the overall amount of the estate to be taxed (and in turn, the amount of estate taxes that will be due from the individual).

When the ILIT has been created, funds may be gifted to the trust in order to cover the amount of the life insurance policy's premium. In order for the gift to qualify for the annual $15,000 (in 2018) per donee gift tax exclusion, the beneficiary (or beneficiaries) of the trust must have the absolute right to withdraw the funds that have been gifted into the trust.

At the death of the insured, the death benefit proceeds from the life insurance policy will be paid to the trust. The trust document will typically include various provisions that outline how the life insurance benefit proceeds may be used.

These provisions could, for example, include an option to purchase assets from the estate, to pay a lump sum or income stream to the insured's beneficiaries, or to loan money to his or her estate for various reasons.

There are any number of reasons to use an irrevocable life insurance trust for estate planning purposes. The primary purpose of many ILITs is to remove the death benefit of a life insurance policy from the gross estate of the grantor. However, a secondary purpose could be to provide liquidity for the owner's gross estate, as well as for the gross estate of other named individuals such as a surviving spouse.

Some people give their annual amount of gift tax exclusion to an ILIT in order to move a certain amount of assets outside of their taxable estate each year. The trustee can then choose to obtain a life insurance policy on the donor's life in order to benefit the trust's beneficiaries.

In other cases, parents or grandparents may create a life insurance trust in order to enhance the value of their estate if they happen to pass away unexpectedly. Because many younger parents have not yet accumulated sizeable estates, the death benefit from the life insurance policy could be used to care for family members in the future should the primary wage earner pass away.

In still other scenarios, an ILIT may be created to offset assets that have been given to a charity. A typical situation could entail someone who makes either a direct gift to a charity or who creates a charitable remainder trust. Because the charity receives the assets at the time of the donor's death rather than family members, an ILIT is set up to benefit the family and to replace the assets.

For those who have larger taxable estates, ILITs can oftentimes replace wealth that would otherwise be lost to estate taxes. Because the death benefit of the life insurance policy will pass directly to trust beneficiaries outside of the deceased person's taxable estate, the money can essentially replace the wealth that would otherwise have been lost to the taxes on the estate.

Trusts can be particularly beneficial for single individuals when planning for efficient, and tax-advantaged, asset transfer. When someone is married, they can automatically transfer all of their assets to their spouse free of taxation. But single people do not have this luxury. So, by setting up the right type of trust, a single person can end up saving 5-, 6-, or even 7-figures in estate taxes, depending on the amount of assets that are being transferred.

Having a trust can also ensure that you will have your healthcare and other financial matters in place, should you become incapacitated in the future and unable to make various decisions on your own.

Chapter 3 Sources

1. Taxable Estate. Investopedia.

2. Ibid.

Chapter 3 Quiz

These quiz questions are here to help you with determining how much of the chapter information you have retained. The answers can be found following the last quiz question in each of the chapters.

1. True or False: You should really have at least $5 million in assets in order to be concerned about estate planning.

2. Which of the following would typically be included in a person's taxable estate?

a. Cash

b. Stocks and bonds

c. Life Insurance

d. All of the Above

3. The total value of one's estate is determined by adding up the total amount of one's _____ and then subtracting the total amount of the estate's _____.

a. assets / liabilities

b. liabilities / assets

c. assets / life insurance

d. investments / losses

4. Having an estate plan will allow you to do which of the following?

a. Protect assets from taxes and creditors

b. Provide control over who receives what, and who doesn't

c. Both a and b

d. Neither a or b

5. When someone dies without having a valid will, they are said to have died
_____.

a. poor

b. rich

c. intestate

d. testate

Chapter 3 Quiz Answers

1. False

2. d

3. a

4. c

5. c

Chapter 4:

The Probate Problem and How to Avoid It

The True Cost of Probate

"Your positive action combined with positive thinking results in success."

Shiv Khera

Many people around the globe are familiar with the long list of hit songs from musician John Denver. Unfortunately, when the singing star died when his single engine plane went down in the Pacific Ocean several years ago, he had no plan in place, leaving his roughly $10 million estate in turmoil.

Because he had no will, Mr. Denver's assets were forced into the probate process, and while there, his estate was challenged more than 30 times. In the end, less than one-third of his estate was left for his surviving spouse and children. To make matters worse, his financial situation was easily accessible in the public records, allowing anyone the ability to view details that most people deem extremely private.

Unfortunately, the situation with John Denver's estate is one that is repeated each and every day, leaving survivors humiliated, frustrated, and oftentimes, with a whole lot less than they would have otherwise received if there was an estate plan in place.

If you've recently become widowed, it is possible that you are all too familiar with this situation. It is also likely that you don't want loved ones to go through the probate process again. And the good news is that with the right type of plan in place, they won't have to.

The Probate Process and Why You Want to Avoid It

Regardless of whether or not you have a will, it is possible that your estate could still be required to go through the process of probate. Many people believe that probate only refers to the administering of the estates of those who do not have wills. But it also includes the process in which your will may be reviewed in order to determine whether it is valid.

During the probate process, the court will appoint either an executor who is named in the will, or if there is no will, it will appoint an administrator of its own choosing, to administer the process of collecting the assets of your estate, paying off your debts, and then distributing the remaining assets to the beneficiaries.

If you have a valid will, the assets *may* go to the named beneficiaries – but this isn't necessarily always the case. If you do not have a valid will, however, the recipients will be determined by the executor. In the latter case, those who are chosen to inherit your assets may not always be your first choice as recipients.

Due to the high legal and court costs, probate can also be fairly expensive - which often leaves much less in terms of assets for your heirs to inherit. It has been estimated that the average cost of probate can be anywhere from 5% to 10% of the gross estate, but in some cases can go as high as 15%.

As most people are likely aware, property and assets for distribution from a decedent can come in any number of forms, such as cash, stocks, bonds, real estate, collectibles, vehicles - and just about anything else.

The probate fee for liquidating assets for disbursal can amount up to 10% or more of the asset's value. Because of this, it could end up that there could virtually be nothing left for heirs once these fees have been incurred. As an example, say that the decedent owned a home that is valued at $1 million, with a $900,000 mortgage balance.

At first glance, it would appear that the heirs would be able to access the $100,000 in equity - but this is not necessarily the case. That's because in some states, the 10% liquidation fee is based on the gross market value of the property. This means that 10% of the home's $1 million market price - which equals $100,000 - would all go into the pocket of the court as the fee, leaving nothing at all for the survivors.

There is also a whole host of other fees that can come from attorneys, the executor(s), and accountants, as well as from taxes that are due, property maintenance fees, and various administrative fees.

On top of the cost, the probate process can also be time consuming, averaging between six and nine months, and sometimes closer to a year to close out an estate. And while this is all going on, survivors are often still left empty-handed.

In addition, there is also a certain amount of publicity that goes along with probate - and not the good kind. Probate is considered to be a public proceeding. This is because any probate file in the courthouse is a matter of public record and is therefore available for public inspection.

This means that all of the assets and liabilities of your probated estate could become a matter of public record. Unfortunately, it isn't just legitimate creditors who can view this information, but also anyone, anywhere can easily gain access to your information.

In fact, there are people who are literally "professional predators" who routinely feast on probate records, many of whom have become quite wealthy by just simply challenging people's probate claims.

In addition, despite people's best intentions, families will oftentimes fight among themselves when someone close to them dies. Probate and related proceedings often end up in disputes. Some of these issues may include:

- Contests of wills and trusts
- Construction (interpretation) of wills and trusts
- Disputed ownership
- Claims for debts or services rendered
- Division of personal property
- Proceedings to retrieve assets from individuals who received them improperly

Here, too, is where a well-documented estate plan can shed light on exactly what your intentions are, eliminating further unrest among family members and allowing them to move forward.

Given all of these negatives, many people will do whatever they can to avoid the probate process. Having a good solid estate plan in place is one of the best ways that you can help to ensure this.

Chapter 4 Quiz

Please complete the Chapter 4 quiz questions. These can assist you with better understanding the key concepts that were covered in this section. The answers may be found directly following the quiz.

1. True or False: Regardless of whether or not you have a will, it is possible that your estate could still be required to go through the process of probate.

2. Which of the following can be used to describe the probate process?

a. costly

b. time-consuming

c. public

d. All of the Above

3. Despite people's best intentions, families will oftentimes fight among themselves when someone close to them dies. Probate and related proceedings often end up in disputes. Just some of these issues may include which of the following:

a. Contests of wills and trusts

b. Disputed ownership

c. Division of personal property

d. All of the Above

4. True or False: If you have a valid will, assets can go to the named beneficiaries.

5. Probate can refer to which of the following?

a. The administering of the estates of those who do not have a will

b. The process in which your will may be reviewed in order to determine whether it is valid

c. Both a and b

d. Neither a or b

Chapter 4 Quiz Answers

1. True

2. d

3. d

4. True

5. c

Chapter 5:

Planning the Next Step of Your Personal Financial Journey

Ensuring Financial Success on Your Own

"Great minds have purposes; others have wishes."

Washington Irving

Over a period of four decades, Julie and her best friend Debra had built up a business empire that included restaurant supply warehousing and delivery, retail, and importing. Now in their 60's, the women each have two children, as well as four grandchildren.

Only one of the adult children, Julie's son Michael, is involved in the business. Over the past couple of years, Julie has been considering stepping down and having Michael take over the company.

However, when she does this, Julie also wants to make sure that there is some financial support provided to her other son, too, as well as Debra's two adult children. Otherwise, Michael could end up inheriting a great deal more than the others, based on the business's current value of roughly $6 million.

Julie also knows that without a clear-cut business succession plan, as well as a personal estate plan, a significant portion of Michael's future wealth could end up in the hands of Uncle Sam, rather than with her loved ones.

With that in mind, Julie and Debra's goal is to create a fair legacy for all of their children, as well as to minimize taxes on their wealth, and to ensure financial security for future generations. Julie decided to meet with an estate planning advisor in order to help her clarify her objectives, and to create a plan. Debra has done the same.

In doing so, the women's advisors worked together and created a comprehensive business transition plan that highlighted the impact of business transition decisions across all aspects of Julie's and Debra's family wealth.

Starting with the fact that Julie and Debra are highly successful business owners, they will likely incur a substantial tax burden if no planning is initiated. Therefore, working with a CPA, the estate planning advisors identified several strategies that would help the business owners to achieve improved after-tax investment returns via income splitting, tax-deferred investing, and the creation of various trusts.

As Julie and Debra would also need to replace their income when they retire, the advisors worked with them in creating tax-efficient individual pension plans. This would assure that both Julie and Debra had a future income stream, and it also allowed the women to currently maximize contributions into the plan.

The advisors also reviewed Julie and Debra's current wills and identified considerations that could be taken into account so as to better ensure that their respective estates would be distributed in a tax-efficient and fair manner.

In terms of leaving a legacy for their grandchildren, the advisors helped Julie and Debra with setting up family trusts for the purpose of education-related savings, as well as with various education payment options that provided much more flexibility than traditional government college savings plans.

Embarking on Your Next Journey in Life

Whether you've found yourself suddenly single due to death or divorce, or even because of retiring from a business that you own, your next "journey" in life will typically require you to make some financial-related changes.

For instance, as a single individual, you may no longer have someone else to rely on for some (or all) of your retirement income. And, when planning ahead for asset transfer situations, single individuals can run into some substantial tax issues if not properly planned for.

As an example, unlike married couples – where one spouse can transfer an unlimited amount of assets tax-free to a surviving spouse – those who are single do not have this luxury. In other words, when transferring any assets or property, Uncle Sam could very well end up being the recipient of a large percentage.

The good news is that there are many viable strategies available that can help to ease the tax burden. And many of these financial planning methods are becoming more common today – especially as single individuals now outnumber married couples in the United States.

While the term "single" indicates that a person is not currently married, there are a number of singles who have been married previously, and who are currently single as the result of divorce or the passing of a spouse.

Based on recent statistics, of unmarried U.S. residents who are age 18 or older, approximately 14% are widowed and 24% are divorced. The other 62% have never been married. Over time, these figures have changed somewhat. For instance, while widow(er)s are becoming less common today, divorce rates are on the rise. Likewise, the percentage of people who have never been married is also rising, and this particular category is nearly double today what it was back in 1960. (1)

Singles By Marital Status

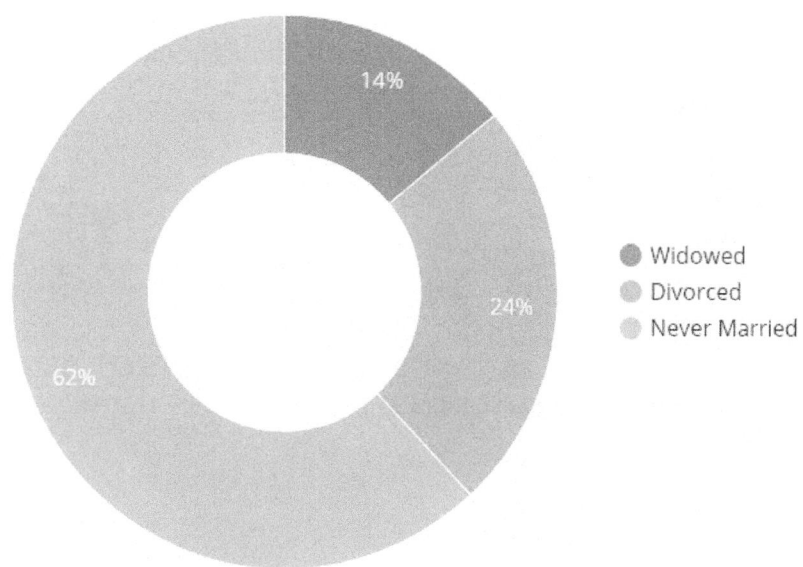

Source: U.S. Singles Statistics. Single Adult Ministry.

Statistics also show that, even though the national population is fairly evenly split between men and women, the singles demographic shows women making up 53%, and men 47%. This equates to roughly 86 unmarried men for every 100 unmarried women.[2]

Contrary to what many people may believe, the growth in the single population isn't centered only on older individuals. In fact, the percentage of singles has nearly tripled in the age 25 to 44 age range since the 1960s. On the other end of the spectrum, there are approximately 17 million unmarried seniors, which accounts for roughly 16% of all U.S. singles.[3]

Singles by Age Group 1960 vs. Now

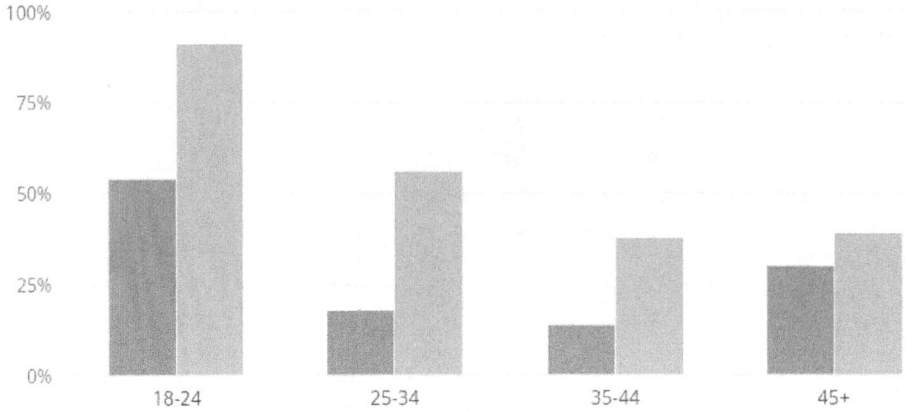

Source: U.S. Singles Statistics. Single Adult Ministry.

The "Problem" with Transferring a Business to a Non-Spouse Beneficiary

While becoming suddenly single due to divorce or death of a spouse can require some significant tax-related planning, the burden of federal and state estate taxes, and inheritance taxes, can fall especially hard on business partner(s), as well as the heirs of a small business owner.

In fact, if you are the owner of a business, your survivors may even be forced to sell your company for the sole purpose of paying the estate taxes. This, in turn, can literally erase all the years of your hard work.

If you and your former spouse or partner were in business together, and you've now suddenly found yourself single, there are a whole host of other issues that you might face in terms of keeping the company afloat during the transition. Likewise, there are several key questions that you need to ask yourself now.

For instance, now that your business partner is no longer here, is your plan to continue keeping the company in operation? Or rather, do you intend to sell the company, or close it down altogether?

Likewise, if you plan to keep the business running, do you now have a succession plan for the company if or when you are no longer able to continue with the day-to-day operation of it yourself?

It is important to note that, if you have recently inherited sole ownership of a business due to divorce or death of your spouse, it is recommended that you not make any significant decisions, at least within the first couple of months.

This can keep you from making more of an emotionally based decision – which could differ from what you really want to happen with your company. In this case, it is oftentimes best to seek the advice of a financial / estate planning professional.

It can also be beneficial to get an idea of the current health and situation of the business that you've fully inherited now. This can lay the foundation for making informed short-term decisions that can help to keep the company intact.

For instance, be sure that you take some time to review important documents, such as the company's:

- Bank statements
- Balance sheet
- Budget
- Business plan
- Debts (loans, credit lines, etc.)

Having a handle on this information can help you with getting a better understanding of the tax, legal, and financial implications of the business transition.

An unexpected business transition can also bring about uncertainty for the company's employees, vendors, and customers. In this case, for example, employees may be shaken by fear of losing their jobs.

Going forward, you also need to ask yourself if owning and running the business on your own is really the right decision for you. Taking on this role on your own may not be easy. So, ask yourself why you truly want to keep hold of the reins.

Here, for instance, do you feel a sense of obligation to the lost spouse or partner that you initially started the business with? Perhaps there are other factors at stake here, too, such as having children and / or other family members as employees. This situation can also add additional pressure for you to stay on as the business's owner. But if this really isn't a responsibility that you want, then you need to also consider the physical and emotional harm that doing so can end up causing.

Unique Financial Planning Issues that Single Business Owners and Entrepreneurs Can Face

Regardless of whether you intend to sell your business outright or keep it running after you are unable (or unwilling) to operate it, careful planning needs to take place in order to ensure that the business will remain up and running during the transition, and that it will be protected from large - and often unexpected - tax liability when transferred or sold.

Believe me, I understand. As a business owner myself for the past several decades, the last thing I want my family and my loyal employees to face is losing their sole source of income if something should happen to me and I'm no longer here to keep things afloat.

Whether you own a small or a large business, there is a good chance that the business is one of your most valuable - if not *the* most valuable - assets that you own. In addition, while the company may be a primary source of income for you, it is likely that it is also a key source of income - and possibly also wealth - for others as well, such as your children (if applicable) and / or your employees.

With that in mind, it is essential to construct an estate plan that covers your company's assets, as well as its organizational structure, and any trade secrets (if applicable) so that events in the future don't have an adverse effect on it.

Continuing Your Business After You're Gone

Tied to estate planning, there are also many reasons that you could need business succession planning. For instance, if the owner of a business dies unexpectedly, their survivors may not be able to efficiently run the business, nor may they have sufficient capital to replace the decedent in his or her particular business role. If you have partners in the company, these partners may or may not have sufficient capital to buy out your share of the business.

In order to help with alleviating this issue, many business succession plans include a buy-sell agreement. These agreements should include provisions for at the very least:

- Death

- Incapacity
- Disability
- Retirement
- Loss of professional licensure
- Failure to perform the expected duties of the business owner
- Bankruptcy

In addition, buy-sell agreements must be funded adequately. In fact, all buy-sell agreements must have provisions in place for the payment of the price of the departing or deceased owner's interest by the surviving owners who will be purchasing the deceased owner's interest in the business.

Some methods used to fund a buy-sell agreement can include:

- An installment sale. This can be determined based on the business's current earnings.
- A fund where a certain amount of capital from the business is invested in order to provide for a future purchase.
- Borrowed funds
- Proceeds from a life insurance policy

Any or all of these, of course, would be dependent on your specific goals and objectives - and, using the right planner who is well-versed in these types of issues, you will be able to essentially "customize" your plan to best meet your wishes.

At an absolute minimum, though, a business estate or succession plan should consist of both ownership and management transfer methods. Ideally, the transfer of business ownership will include the following:

- Consideration of what is in the best interest of the business and those who depend on it for their financial support
- A valuation of the company
- Timing of the transfer

Likewise, the succession of your company management should consist of the following:

- Delegating the responsibility - including proper authority - to the company's successors
- The development and training of the successors
- Methods of retaining key employees of the business

In addition, there should also be steps that are taken to help in minimizing taxes and avoiding the probate process should the business transfer take place following your passing. In many ways, this can be accomplished in a similar fashion as that of individual estate planning techniques.

Chapter 5 Sources

1. U.S. Singles Statistics. Single Adult Ministry.

2. Ibid.

3. Ibid.

Chapter 5 Quiz

Please complete the quiz questions for Chapter 5. These will help you with retaining the important points that were covered in this section. Answers to the quiz questions can be found immediately after Question 5.

1. True or False: The burden of estate taxes can fall particularly hard on the heirs of a small business owner.

2. True or False: Unlike married couples – where one spouse can transfer an unlimited amount of assets tax-free to a surviving spouse – those who are single do not have this luxury?

3. A business buy-sell agreement does not need to address which of the following:

a. death

b. incapacity

c. retirement

d. None of the Above (i.e., this agreement should address all of these issues)

4. The succession of company management should consist of which of the following:

a. Methods of retaining key employees of the business

b. The development and training of the successors

c. Delegating the responsibility to the company's successors

d. All of the Above

5. True or False: In many ways, the steps that are taken for minimizing taxes and avoiding the probate process for business owners can be accomplished in a similar manner to that of individual estate planning techniques.

Chapter 5 Quiz Answers

1. True

2. True

3. d

4. d

5. True

Chapter 6:

Keeping Your Promises and Ensuring You Will Always Be Remembered

How to Leave a Legacy on Your Terms

"Our goals can only be reached through a vehicle of a plan in which we must fervently believe, and upon which we must vigorously act. There is no other route to success."

Pablo Picasso

Roger, a 65-year-old doctor from India who currently lives in Chicago, knows the value of a good education. He often reflects on how blessed he is to have had the opportunity to attend medical school, which in turn, led him to build up a thriving practice.

So, it stands to reason that when asked by his financial advisor what his biggest goal was, Roger said that he had always wanted to send ten students to medical school back home in India each year for the rest of his life. Unfortunately, Roger stated, nobody had been able to show him how to accomplish this.

After considering all of the aspects of Roger's goal, his advisor came back to him with a viable plan. Using a lifetime annuity, not only would Roger be able to forge ahead with helping ten students each year, but he could do so by simply forwarding $800,000 over a period of time to a 501c3 and using the income from that investment to continue financing his goal for years to come.

When the time came for Roger to write the first $100,000 check to contribute to the plan, he literally began to cry tears of joy, as he imagined countless young doctors entering the field throughout the years.

Multi-generational Wealth Creation Strategies

You are likely familiar with the phrase, "You can't take it with you when you go." So, with that in mind, it is important that you do whatever you can while you're still here to maintain control of your assets, as well as delegate who will benefit from your life's work in the future.

Failing to make any type of provisions for who gets what when you're gone can create significant obstacles when the time comes - and it is likely that taxes and other costs, such as probate, will consume a majority of your estate.

This can be the case regardless of whether you are single or married. In fact, many single individuals forgo multi-generational wealth transfer strategies, feeling that it just isn't important. But the reality is that wealth transfer can often be even more important for those who are not married, as a large percentage of your hard-earned assets could be lost to taxes.

For those who plan to pass most or all of your assets to a surviving spouse, the process is fairly straightforward. That's because a spouse can receive 100% of their deceased spouse's assets free of estate taxation.

However, when the time comes for single individuals to pass wealth on to a subsequent generation, Uncle Sam and other creditors could end up being the biggest beneficiary unless you have planned otherwise.

Even if you don't have children, there are likely other loved ones in your life, and / or a favorite charity, who could benefit substantially from a financial boost. So, you want to make sure that you have a plan in place that will reduce, or even eliminate, taxes when you pass these assets on.

In doing so, there are several key ways to protect transferred assets from your creditors and the tax man. These can include:

- Outright Gifts. One option is to make outright gifts. Giving outright gifts of assets is a very common way of passing on wealth. This method can also help to protect the transferred assets from your creditors. When you go this route, though, keep in mind that you will lose all economic interest in the assets, as well as any and all control over them permanently, as soon as you gift the assets away.
- Irrevocable Life Insurance Trust (ILIT). As previously discussed, another option for removing assets from your estate and protecting them from creditors is through the use of an Irrevocable Life Insurance Trust, or ILIT. This type of trust protects the cash value in life insurance from creditors during your lifetime – and it further protects the policy's proceeds when you pass on.
- Qualified Personal Residence Trust (QPRT). A Qualified Personal Residence Trust, or QPRT, will let you transfer a primary or vacation residence to a trust while you reserve the right to live in the home for a term of years. The value of the interest that you retain (that is, the right to live in the house for a term of years) is calculated using IRS tables.

  The value of the property that is transferred into the trust, minus your term interest's value, is a gift that is known as the "remainder interest." This gift can be sheltered from gift tax by your gift tax exemption. If you survive the term of years, the trust is not included in your estate for estate tax purposes. QPRTs essentially provide protection from creditors by insulating the residence from your creditors' claims. In a creditor protection situation, the non-debtor spouse should create the QPRT and retain the term interest.

- Charitable Remainder Trust (CRT). For a donor, one of the primary ideal behind a Charitable Remainder Trust, or CRT, is to reduce taxes. This is done by first donating assets into the trust and then having the trust pay the named beneficiary for a set period of time. Once the time period has expired, the remainder of the estate is transferred to the charity (or charities) that are deemed as beneficiaries.

Even if you already have a will in place, as previously discussed, this is typically not enough to keep your assets adequately protected from taxes, creditors, and other potential risks. Therefore, a trust may also be necessary - particularly when you consider the following:

#1: Wills versus Trusts: When Each Takes Effect

The fundamental difference between a will and a trust is that your will is executed on your passing, and a trust goes into effect as soon as it is set up and signed. Both can be altered and amended before your death, as long as you are considered to be mentally competent. The only exception to changes being made to your beneficiaries or to distributions is if you have set up an irrevocable living trust with which you forfeit this right as part of the trust's terms.

#2 Wills versus Trusts: The Assets Each Covers

It is only possible for your last will and testament to allow for the distribution of assets that are owned only in your name. Because of that, jointly held assets such as real estate, as well as life insurance policies, fall outside of the governance of your will.

On the other hand, a trust has governance over all the assets that it has been funded with. You have the freedom to add assets into it after it is created - which can include assets that you hold jointly with others. Here, the heirs that you select will benefit from your percentage or proportion of joint assets, rather than the value of its entirety.

#3: Wills versus Trusts: Trusts Provide for You in Life and Death

If you are retired or you are approaching retirement, it is important to know that trusts can provide for your family through your golden years - and beyond. With a will, it is not possible to build in protection against a physical or cognitive impairment in later years, as it does not come into effect until after you have passed. A trust provides you with an extra cushion of protection against worst case future health scenarios.

#4: Wills versus Trusts: Benefits for Single Individuals

If you are single and you have assets that are held solely in your name, then a trust is typically preferable to a will. This is because with a trust, your assets can avoid probate - leaving your loved ones burdened with extra costs - and you can avoid going into court-supervised guardianship if you should become incapacitated. A trust ensures that your beneficiaries get the maximum from your estate, whereas a will can devastate it in the name of Uncle Sam.

#5: Wills versus Trusts: Benefits for Those Who Have Minor Beneficiaries

Parents who have young children are advised to make provisions for any minors who are dependent on them so that they are taken care of if the parent(s) passes away. In many cases, the largest asset you have is either your life insurance or the money in your retirement fund - and in cases where you only have a will, these assets will be placed into a court-supervised guardianship if your beneficiary is a minor at the time of the parent's death.

The assets under supervision will be used for the benefit of the child(ren) until the time they turn age 18, and then the child(ren) will inherit the remaining capital, often with significant tax implications.

In contrast, a trust can be named as a beneficiary of your life insurance and / or your retirement plan (such as your 401k and / or IRA), so that the funds are transferred to your heir directly, rather than through a court-supervised guardian. With a trust, you are also able to specify when you want children to receive their inheritance, such as at age 25 or 30, as versus at age 18.

#6: Wills versus Trusts: Estate Taxes and Married Couples

The federal estate tax exemption is set at $11.2 million per individual (in 2018). This means that an individual may leave up to this amount to heirs and not have to pay federal estate or gift tax. Married couples can also pass an unlimited amount to one another, upon the death of the first spouse.

Even if you were once married, but you are widowed now, if your estate exceeds $11.2 million, you can run into estate tax issues. But a trust can make it possible to protect your assets from devastation from estate taxation if you are a single individual.

#7: Wills versus Trusts: Second or Later Marriages

If you plan to marry, or remarry, it is possible that you and your future spouse may each have different beneficiaries. In this case, a trust is highly recommended over just a will in terms of planning because the trust allows each spouse to specify who inherits what from the estate. In addition, assets will be inherited outside of the probate process, making for a smoother distribution of your wealth.

#8: Wills versus Trusts: Maintaining Your Privacy

Not many people are aware that a last will and testament is on public record. This means that anyone - including those who may try to obtain a piece of your estate, such as predators and / or disgruntled ex-partners - can view the in-depth information about your assets.

A trust, however, is completely private. Therefore, having a trust can allow your financial situation to be known only to those who you want it to be. In addition, it can also work well for you if there are any disputes or claims against your state after your death.

#9: Wills versus Trusts: Ownership of Property Outside Your State

A trust is also highly recommended if you own real estate outside of your state of residence. In this situation, if you have only a will, your family will likely face "ancillary", or separate probate in each state that you have registered ownership of property. Trusts, however, can mitigate this significantly by keeping all of your assets in the same place.

#10: No Estate is "Too Small" to Consider Planning with Trusts

Estate planning is a complex business, regardless of how wealthy you are. Even with an average retirement pot of around $100,000 it is well worth strategizing with trusts if you have dependents who are counting on you.

You can also use trusts during life, too, such as providing you with a solid income through your retirement that won't be ravaged by the tax man. So, while you may think that trust funds are the stuff of only wealthy people, the reality is that they are also the stuff of regular families who have the foresight to plan ahead.[1]

Leaving a Legacy on Your Terms

You don't need to live in a mansion or drive a Rolls Royce in order to leave a legacy to those you love. In fact, there are many ways in which you can ensure that future generations, charities, and / or other recipients will continue to know, love, and remember you.

Whether it is in the form of an inheritance for your loved ones, a donation to your church or favorite charity, and / or an endowment for your former college or university, you can leave a legacy that you're proud of - and you can do it on your terms. In order to do so successfully, though, it takes a well thought out plan.

The whole purpose of estate planning is to allow you to get the most enjoyment from your assets during your lifetime, and then to pass whatever is left to the ones you love, with the least possible shrinkage of value.

Setting up a trust is important because it limits the devastation that can be caused by estate taxes and other associated expenses upon your passing. It also gives you complete control over how your assets are distributed so that others are not placed into a higher tax bracket.

In addition, minors can be guaranteed a long-term income source, and if you have any heirs with bad financial behaviors, these individuals can be prevented from quickly dwindling their inheritance. Trusts can also serve as protection against lawsuits from predators or ex-partners, ensuring that the beneficiaries you name are the only recipients of your assets.

While we may not like to think about it, at some point, each and every one of us will pass away. What we can't say, though, is when that will occur. With that in mind, getting a plan in place sooner rather than later is the key to your financial success - both now and in the future.[2]

Chapter 6 Sources

1. Top 10 Things You Must Know Before Considering a Will or Trust. FRA Trust.

2. Ibid.

Chapter 6 Quiz

It is time now to complete the quiz for Chapter 6. The answers can be found following the last question of the quiz.

1. Your spouse can receive _____% of your assets free of estate taxation.

a. 25%

b. 50%

c. 75%

d. 100%

2. True or False: Failing to make any type of provisions for who gets what when you're gone can create significant obstacles when the time comes - and it is likely that taxes and other costs, such as probate, will consume a majority of your estate.

3. A _____ allows you to transfer significant sums of tax-free cash to beneficiaries who are at least two generations younger than you.

a. family trust

b. Family Limited Partnership

c. dynasty trust

d. None of the Above

4. A(n) _____ protects the cash value of life insurance policies from creditors during your lifetime, and further protects the policies' proceeds when you pass on.

a. ILIT

b. CRT

c. GRAT

d. None of the Above

5. True or False: The fundamental difference between a will and a trust is that your will is executed on your passing, and a trust goes into effect as soon as it is set up and signed.

Chapter 6 Quiz Answers

1. d

2. True

3. c

4. a

5. True

Chapter 7:

Making Sure You Fill in All the Gaps (or What Could Possibly Go Wrong?)

Protection from the Long List of Threats to Your Financial Plan

"No one's ever achieved financial fitness with a January resolution that's abandoned by February."

Suze Orman

When John's father passed away, John - an only child - was named as the sole heir to his estate. Unfortunately, though, the estate included more than $50,000 in credit card debt, and a home that had negative equity.

Although John had read that typically, personal debt "dies" along with the borrower, the reality is that as with all things financial, there are exceptions. For example, a lot can depend on how the assets are titled.

There is also the question of whether or not there were any guarantors on the debt. Therefore, in certain cases, an heir could very well become stuck with the debt. In this case, John had co-signed on a recent auto loan for his father, and in doing so, he essentially made a commitment to pay off that loan on his father's behalf if his dad was no longer able to.

Due to the large amount of debt that was associated with his father's estate, the executor sold off all items of value in order to pay the creditors. This, in turn, left nothing at all for John - other than a substantial amount of time in sorting things out.

The Potential Threats to Your Financial Plan

Even if you've saved and invested well all of your life, there are numerous threats that can befall your financial plan - some of which are in your control, and others that are not. One of the most common of these can include a health care or long-term care need.

Health / Long-Term Care Need

For any number of different reasons, an individual may become unable to manage their medical and financial decisions effectively and may at some point need the assistance of another person in order to do so.

In fact, it only makes sense to assume that as you age, you are likely to become more vulnerable to chronic illness. And unfortunately, this can be difficult physically, as well as from a financial standpoint.

As a single individual, is there someone that you can rely on to be your caregiver?

If not, then you may need to hire someone to provide you with the assistance that you need. Unfortunately, long-term care costs can add much more to the health care expense responsibility - even if you just simply require assistance with basic activities of daily living, such as bathing or dressing, and you receive these services in your own home.

Knowing the approximate costs of different types of care can help you to better plan for them. Based on the Genworth 2017 Cost of Care Survey (conducted by Carescout), the national median monthly care costs in 2017 include:

- Adult Day Health Care - $1,517 per month
- Assisted Living Facility - $3,750 per month
- Homemaker Services - $3,994 per month
- Home Health Aide - $4,099 per month
- Semi-Private Room in a Skilled Nursing Facility - $7,148 per month
- Private Room in a Skilled Nursing Facility - $8,121 per month[2]

Depending on the type of care that you need, you could see expenses of nearly $100,000 per year - and if both you and your spouse require care, the figures could double. And these are in today's dollars.

Nursing homes are becoming increasingly expensive, with an average price increase of nearly 4% per year for more than 20 years. So, if you don't actually require care for many years, the charges can be that much more.

With that in mind, it is essential to have a plan in place for health care, disability, and incapacity. This includes having a financial safety net, as well as an individual (or individuals) who you can rely upon to make decisions for you if you become unable to do so for yourself.

For example, a person is considered incompetent to the extent that he or she lacks sufficient understanding or capacity to make or to communicate responsible decisions with regard to his or her personal care and / or financial affairs. When this is the case, it is always best to have pre-planned in advance for both medical and financial needs going forward.

When you're approaching retirement, or even if you are already in retirement and you are addressing your estate planning needs, it is also a good time to make sure that you have the mechanisms in place to take care of any unexpected health care costs if your health should decline in the future.

In the absence of pre-planning for incompetence, each state provides a court ordered arrangement that is governed by state law. For example, "guardianship" is the general term that is used for the arrangement that involves responsibility for both the person and the property of one who has been judged as being incompetent.

Once appointed, the guardian will deal with the "ward's" personal living decisions and property with many of the same rights that the ward would have, if he or she were competent. However, in dealing with the ward's property, the combination of state law and fiduciary standards severely restricts investment options, use of assets, and disbursement of funds.

Essentially, every power and duty that is given to a guardian basically deprives the ward of his or her basic civil and property rights, such as the right to control their own living arrangements and daily activities, the right to write checks, the right to make gifts, the right to contract, and the right to buy and sell property.

In the event of no pre-planning for incapacity, individuals give up a great deal of control over what happens with their assets, as well as even their most basic choices in life such as their living arrangements, basic activities, and in some cases, even who their care provider will be.

How to Plan for the Worst (Even While Hoping for the Best)

In planning for a possible incapacity down the road, there are several strategies that can be used in order to better protect your assets, as well as to make sure that the assets and property will continue being managed in the manner you would like them to be. These strategies can also include how decisions will be made for your healthcare needs going forward.

Some of these strategies include the following:

Durable Power of Attorney

One approach to help ensure that your financial needs will be met is to set up a durable power of attorney. In its most basic sense, a power of attorney is defined as "a legal document that gives someone you choose the power to act in your place."

In case you ever become mentally incapacitated, you will need what are known as "durable" powers of attorney for your finances (and also your medical care). A durable power of attorney simply means that the document stays in effect if you become incapacitated and you are not able to handle matters on your own. (This is as versus "nondurable" powers of attorney that automatically end if a person who makes them loses mental capacity).[3]

State law specifies the requisite capacity that is needed to execute a power of attorney. Such laws typically involve the principal's ability to understand the character of the transaction or the nature and consequences of his or her acts.

The power of attorney creates what is known as an "agency" relationship between one person (the "principal") and another person or institution (the "attorney in fact"). The scope of the authority that is granted to the attorney in fact by the written document may be limited.

For example, it may allow the power to perform only one specific act, such as selling a specific asset or property. Or, it may be broad and allow the attorney in fact to perform any act that the principal can perform - other than executing a will.

It is important to note that the actions that are taken by the attorney in fact pursuant to the terms of the instrument are legally binding on the principal. Also, while a durable power of attorney remains valid at the principal's incapacity, it ceases at the principal's death.

Medical Power of Attorney

In general, a medical power of attorney - also referred to as a durable power of attorney for health care - is one type of health care directive. It is a document that sets out your wishes for health care if you are ever too ill or injured to speak for yourself.

When creating a medical power of attorney, you name a trusted person to oversee your medical care and to make health care decisions for you if you are not able to do so on your own. Depending on where you reside, the person that you appoint may be referred to as your agent, your attorney in fact, your health care proxy, your health care surrogate, or a similar term.

The health care agent will work with your doctors and other health care providers in making sure that you receive the type of medical care that you wish to receive. When arranging your care, the agent is legally bound to follow your treatment preferences to the extent that he or she knows about them.

In order to make your wishes clear, you can use a second type of health care directive, which is oftentimes referred to as a health care declaration or a living will, to provide written health care instructions to your agent and health care providers.

How can you best go about appointing an agent for your power of attorney?

Whoever you choose to be your agent will carry a considerable amount of responsibility - particularly if you are granting powers to manage your financial matters. This is why your selection should be carefully considered, and that the chosen person or entity be one that you trust implicitly to carry out your wishes if you are not able to do so yourself.

You can appoint anyone who is over the age of 18 to be your agent. So, if you have a niece, nephew, friend, or other loved one who you trust will do a good job, they could be considered. There are some items to be mindful of, though, when choosing who will be your agent.

For instance, sometimes it is the people who are the closest to you who may find the subject of your possible future ill health to be too distressing to discuss in any depth. They may also be fearful of the overwhelming responsibility of what you are asking of them.

For this reason, it can oftentimes be best to choose someone who is less emotionally connected to you, as they may be better qualified to carry out their ultimate duties as your power of attorney.

It is also fairly common for a person's situation and circumstances to change. Therefore, it is always a good idea to choose a backup agent, too. That way, if for whatever reason your first choice is unable to carry out their duties, you will still be assured that there is someone on standby to make sure that you receive the care you requested, in the way that you requested it.

Living Will

Most commonly, living wills are used to state a person's desire to be allowed to die without the application of life-prolonging artificial measures. However, a living will can also be used for requesting certain types of treatment or pain relief.

Specifically, a living will should inform doctors, nurses, and other medical professionals whether procedures such as artificial respiration or ventilation, heart pumping, dialysis, certain painkilling medications, and artificial feeding should be administered or withheld.

Very specific instructions are important here because, in many states, if a person does not specify his or her exact preferences, the state statute will direct the health care provider to follow a certain course of action that may or may not be the same as the individual's personal wishes.

With that in mind, a good living will should ideally lay out under what circumstances the individual wants certain procedures administered or withheld. Oftentimes, state law will specify the conditions that will trigger the treatment provisions of a person's living will - and often, an incompetent person's condition must be terminal, incurable, or possibly chronic. There are also usually certain formalities that will need to be followed in order for a living will to be considered valid. And, a certain number of witnesses are usually required as well.

A living will details your wishes with regard to whether or not you want to be kept alive using medical means such as, for instance, with a breathing tube. These documents can work in conjunction with other advance medical directives such as medical powers of attorney, which can authorize someone to make medical decisions on your behalf if you aren't able to do so. Living wills typically take precedence over medical powers of attorney.

Healthcare Proxy

A healthcare proxy is a type of advance medical directive - which is a legal document - that will designate another person, or "proxy," to make health care decisions in case you become incapable of making your own wishes known. Here, the healthcare proxy will essentially have the same rights to either refuse or request treatment that you do if you were capable of communicating your desires.

Maintaining Control with a Revocable / Living Trust

While a revocable living trust is included in many estate plans, these entities can also be used as an effective tool in planning for one's incapacity. In order to implement this strategy, the trust's grantor would create a revocable trust that is immediately funded.

In doing so, the grantor - who is typically also the trustee - would change the title on all of the appropriate property by making the revocable living trust the holder of legal title to the property. The trust's document will specify what happens if and when the grantor becomes incapacitated or dies.

Should incapacity occur, the grantor would then be removed as the trustee and full trust powers could then be granted to either a co-trustee or to a successor trustee, who will then continue to manage the property in the trust according to the provisions in the trust's document.

A living trust allows you to take the reins of your health care decisions ahead of your need to implement them. It also ensures that your wishes are communicated if you should find yourself in a situation where you are unable to communicate them yourself.

This can be an advantage to your loved ones in particular, as they will be relieved of the responsibility of making your important health care decisions for you - which can oftentimes create upset and division among family members.

When setting up a living trust and dealing with the aspect of your care in cases of chronic illness or disability, it is always good to talk things over with your family so that it is clear that this is how you would like to proceed if or when the time comes.

Long-Term Care Insurance / Disability Insurance

You may also want to consider long-term care insurance or a disability policy. These policies can help you to pay for some (or even all) of the care that you receive, either in a facility or at home. There are multiple ways to do this - and these policies can be somewhat confusing - so it is best to discuss your potential options with a knowledgeable professional.

Given the steep price tag today on even the most basic types of care, having insurance coverage can help to better ensure that you won't have to dip into savings or other assets that are already earmarked for other needs.

Having a plan in place to cover long-term care, as well as a possible disabling situation, is particularly beneficial for single individuals. One of the biggest reasons for this is because you don't have a spouse's income (including retirement income and Social Security income) to rely upon if you are unable to work, and / or if you require long-term care.

With that in mind, make sure that you have a good estimate of what your expenses will be going forward, and then plan to cover those with a good, solid plan. This can allow you to focus on your health, rather than worrying about whether or not you will be able to continue paying your bills.

Planning Ahead for Special Needs

We have many clients who have benefitted from Special Needs Trusts. For example, Jay, a widowed father of three grown children - one of which is a 26-year-old daughter with special needs.

Jay has been a Major in the United States Air Force for many years - and, due good life-long savings habits, he and his late wife had accumulated roughly $3 million in assets. When we initially met with Jay, however, he had no will in place, nor had he done any type of estate or wealth planning.

He did want to ensure, though, that all three of his children would inherit a nice sum when he was gone, and that his special needs daughter would be taken care of for the remainder of her life.

Therefore, we suggested that Jay secure a $2.7 million life insurance policy that would pay out at his passing, with the proceeds going to his daughter, and that the remainder of his other assets would go to his other two children. That way, once the estate is settled, all three of Jay's children would be equally taken care of financially.

Once this plan was in place, the otherwise staunch Jay started to get very emotional, telling us that he had not previously realized what he could do for his daughter, as well as for his other children. He finally had the peace of mind that he had been looking for.

So how exactly can a special needs trust help?

For starters, these types of trusts can actually be set up in order to provide for an incapacitated individual's extra needs - other than basic food, shelter, and health care expenses - that may be covered by public assistance benefits that the person is entitled to receive under certain programs such as Medicaid or SSI (Supplemental Security Income).

Here, the grantor will typically create and fund an irrevocable trust for the benefit of someone else, such as a parent for a special needs child or an adult child for an older parent. The trustee is usually given discretionary power over the distribution of the trust's income and principal for the benefit of the trust's beneficiary.

Although the terms can vary, the trustee can oftentimes have sole discretion over the income and principal in the trust in order to maximize the beneficiary's eligibility for public assistance benefits. The trust could also allow the trustee to terminate the trust if it is possible that the ward may in the future become competent again and able to manage his or her own assets.

It is important to be careful when funding and creating a Special Needs Trust, as allowing the grantor to retain too much control over trust distributions, or if trust income is used to discharge a legal support obligation, the income could become taxable to him or her.

Other Threats to Your Estate that Should Be Planned For

While death, disability, and incapacity can be substantial threats to your estate, these aren't the only dangers that may be lurking. Some of the other factors that could reduce assets that go to your heirs include creditors / unpaid debts, and / or lawsuits.

Generally, when an individual dies, his or her estate will be responsible for paying their debts. This means that, as with the case above of John and his father, the executor of the decedent's estate may need to sell all assets that have value in order to help with paying off the debt. This, in turn, could leave nothing at all for heirs.

Another big threat to one's estate is getting sued. This is particularly the case for those who are business owners or medical professionals. By the time you are hit with a lawsuit, it is likely much too late to protect yourself, your heirs, or your assets. Therefore, it is important to act ahead of time and implement an asset protection plan.

One of the other primary threats to your estate is having assets end up somewhere that you didn't intend them to. For example, many people name their spouse as a beneficiary on life insurance policies and retirement plans.

But if the marriage doesn't work out, unless you remove your ex's name from these assets, guess what will happen - he or she will still be the beneficiary. There are numerous reasons why this is just plain bad planning, and why any financial or estate plan needs to be reviewed on a regular basis.

Chapter 7 Sources

1. Retiree health care costs continue to surge. Fidelity Viewpoints. September 6, 2017. (https://www.fidelity.com/viewpoints/retirement/retiree-health-costs-rise)

2. Compare Long Term Care Costs Across the United States. Genworth Cost of Care Survey 2017. (https://www.genworth.com/about-us/industry-expertise/cost-of-care.html)

3. www.nolo.com

Chapter 7 Quiz

Please go through the short Chapter 7 quiz in order to determine how much you have retained from this section. You may find the correct answers following these five Chapter 7 questions.

1. _____ is the general term that is used for the arrangement that involves responsibility for both the person and the property of one who has been judged as being incompetent.

a. intestate

b. guardianship

c. executor

d. beneficiary

2. True or False: When you are constructing an estate plan, it is typically not necessary to address potential health care and / or long-term care needs.

3. A(n) _____ is defined as "a legal document that gives someone you choose the power to act in your place."

a. estate plan

b. ILIT

c. durable power of attorney

d. None of the Above

4. Most commonly, a(n) _____ are used to state a person's desire to be allowed to die without the application of life-prolonging artificial measures. However, it can also be used for requesting certain types of treatment or pain relief.

a. power of attorney

b. durable power of attorney

c. living will

d. estate plan

5. True or False: Generally, when an individual dies, his or her estate will be responsible for paying their debts.

Chapter 7 Quiz Answers

1. b

2. False

3. c

4. c

5. True

Chapter 8:

Making Sense of Alphabet Soup - The Tools Used in the Estate Planning Process

Understanding the Available Tools and How to Use Them

"Don't wish it were easier; wish you were better."

Jim Rohn

Beth, age 38, was the mother of a 12-year-old son. While she wasn't really a good saver, Beth did have a $1 million investment account in her name based on funds that were received years earlier from a wrongful death settlement.

Even though Beth had a simple will that left everything to her young son, she had put off doing any type of major financial planning, feeling that she was "too young" to worry about it - and besides, she thought, all of those fancy trusts and strategies are really only for the very wealthy and those who understand all of the confusing jargon.

Unfortunately, Beth was killed instantly in an auto accident, and her son, who was also in the vehicle with her, passed just a few hours later in the hospital. The only other heir that Beth's son had was his father - who was never really involved in his life and was a drug addict. In this situation, all of Beth's assets passed to her son (because she died first), and then at the son's death, all of his assets passed on to his biological father. Beth's family, however, received nothing at all.

Had Beth taken the time to set up a trust, leaving the trust assets to her son and also naming a contingent beneficiary in case her son passed away, the son's father would not have received anything, and the assets would have instead gone to Beth's parents and her two younger sisters.

Tools and Strategies to Use for Asset Protection

Sometimes the biggest incentive to moving forward with getting your estate plan completed is hearing stories about what has happened with other people - and in turn, creating a way to avoid such situations.

Although estate planning can certainly be somewhat complicated, your advisors should counsel and advise you regarding the best ways to accomplish your estate planning goals and objectives. With that in mind, you should feel comfortable talking with your advisors about your goals, questions, and concerns.

Asset protection involves a set of techniques that are designed for protecting the assets of individuals and businesses from loss. These can include - but are by far not limited only to - civil litigation, legal issues involving taxation, ill-conceived investments, probate, and a whole host of other items.

Many people are under the misconception that asset protection is strictly for the wealthy. But the reality is that anyone who has anything to protect should understand

and follow the strategies that are outlined here in order to protect what they've worked for.

In a nutshell, estate planning is the process of accumulating, preserving, and distributing assets in order to achieve your financial goals during your lifetime, and to provide for your heirs according to your wishes at death.

These goals and objectives may include some or all of the following:

- Providing for family cash and income needs in the event of your death
- Establishing a child's future college education fund
- Planning for a financially secure retirement
- Providing funds in the event of your illness or disability
- Planning for the special needs of a disabled child or other family member
- Establishing a plan for the orderly disposition of business interests in the event of your disability or death
- Implementing a program of lifetime giving to family members
- Making meaningful contributions to a favorite charity

Estate planning is not just a one-time event, but rather it is an ongoing process that is designed to accomplish accumulation, preservation, and distribution objectives, both during your life and following your death.

Tools and Trusts Used in Estate Planning Strategies

There are a wide variety of tools that are used in the estate planning process - and each can provide various benefits, depending on one's circumstances, needs, and ultimate goals. Some of the primary vehicles include the following:

Life Insurance

Life insurance proceeds can be used in a variety of ways in the estate planning process, such as for the needs of surviving family members, creating needed liquidity to pay estate settlement costs, equalizing inheritances among family members, retaining a business interest among family members, and / or making substantial charitable donations. Given that, careful consideration should be given to life insurance ownership and beneficiary arrangements.

Do you want to protect assets and heirs without having to actually fund the life insurance premiums yourself?

You can if you finance the premium. As its name implies, life insurance premium financing involves taking out a third-party loan to pay for a policy's premiums. As with other types of loans, the lender will charge interest, and you - the borrower - repay the loan in regular installments, until the debt is satisfied, or until the insured passes away, in which case the loan balance is typically paid off via the life insurance proceeds.[1]

Why consider financing your premium as versus just paying it yourself?

There are actually some very viable reasons for doing so. First, if you're considering a life insurance policy with a face value in the millions or the tens of millions of dollars, the premium could easily cost upwards of $100,000 per year.

Therefore, financing the premium can make a lot of since, as it allows people to borrow at a competitive rate, while keeping the money you would have spent in investments that yield a higher rate of return. Also, premium financing can help to prevent you from triggering capital gains taxes if you have to liquidate assets in order to pay for the premium out-of-pocket.[2]

Annuities

An annuity is technically defined as a type of contract that is between an individual and an insurance company. This contract can guarantee a stream of income to the person on whose life is based on this contract – otherwise known as the annuitant - in return for either a lump sum deposit or periodic contributions from the annuity holder into the contract.

The interest that occurs inside of an annuity is income tax deferred until it is either paid out or withdrawn. This tax-deferral can allow the funds inside the annuity to grow and compound exponentially over time.

Annuities may be structured in a variety of different ways with regard to the manner that they are funded, as well as in how – and for how long - they pay out income to the annuitant. This gives annuity purchasers a great deal of flexibility in setting up the contract to meet their specific needs.

There are two primary phases in the life of an annuity. These include the accumulation phase and the payout phase. It is during the accumulation phase that the annuity is funded by its holder.

Annuity owners have a choice in how they decide to fund their annuity contract. In some instances, an annuity may be funded with one lump sum. In other cases, the annuity owner may decide to fund the contract through a series of regular or sporadic contributions.

One of the distinguishing features of an annuity is whether it is fixed or variable. Although both types may be funded in a similar fashion, and both offer like payout options, there is a definite difference in how these two types of annuity products operate.

For instance, a fixed annuity typically offers its holder a fixed amount of interest that is credited on an annual basis. The interest rate is declared by the insurance company that offers the annuity.

The primary benefit to a fixed annuity is its safety of principal that allows the owner of these products the peace of mind in knowing that they will not lose money - regardless of what occurs in the stock market. In return for this safety of principal, though, the return on fixed annuities is typically somewhat low.

Variable annuities are set up in a similar fashion to fixed annuities. However, these products allow their holders to participate in stock market appreciation with their funds through a number of different investment options, such as mutual funds. These underlying investments are typically held in "sub-accounts."

Those who own a variable annuity have the potential to grow their account a great deal, provided that the underlying investments perform well. Conversely, these types of annuities may also be considered much riskier than fixed annuities, due primarily to the potential of poor market returns on their investments.

Today, investors also have the option to purchase indexed annuities. These annuities have their return based primarily on the performance of an underlying market index such as the S&P 500. For example, if the underlying index performs well during a given year, then a positive return is produced for the annuity - oftentimes up to a certain stated maximum, or "cap."

And here's where indexed annuities really shine. If the underlying index performs poorly during a given year, the annuity is simply credited with a 0%. So, while there is no gain, there is also no loss for that period, in turn, keeping principal protected.

The opportunity to receive a guaranteed lifetime income from an annuity is also a key feature - especially given our longer average life expectancy today. This ongoing income stream can help to ensure that you won't run out of money during your lifetime - and if you choose the joint life income option, you and your spouse can count on income for the remainder of both of your lives.

Grantor Retained Annuity Trusts

A grantor retained annuity trust, also referred to as a GRAT, is a gift of a remainder interest in an irrevocable trust, under which the grantor has retained an annuity interest for a term of years. This particular strategy can minimize tax liability that exists when intergenerational transfers of estate assets occur.

Using a GRAT, an irrevocable trust is established for a certain period of time. The person who establishes the trust pays a tax when the trust is created. Assets are placed under the trust, and then an annuity is paid out each year.

The annuity amount can be expressed as either a fixed dollar amount or as a fixed percentage of the initial fair market value of the trust assets. However, the trust may provide that the grantor is entitled to income of the trust in excess of the annuity amount.

At the time the grantor retained annuity trust expires, the beneficiary of the trust will then receive the trust's assets tax free. If, however, the person who established the trust dies before the trust expires, the assets will become a part of his or her taxable estate, and the beneficiary will not receive anything.[3]

Charitable Remainder Trusts

A charitable remainder trust, or CRT, is a type of trust that can be included in a person's estate plan that allows the gifting of assets in the present time - while still receiving income, as well as estate tax benefits.

CRTs are tax exempt trust instruments that allow the trust's donor to make current gifts of assets or property into the trust, while at the same time retaining the ability to keep an income stream from those assets.

Once a charitable remainder trust has been set up, cash or other types of assets can be placed into it. Typically, the trust will name the donor - as well as the donor's spouse, if applicable - as the beneficiary of income. This means that the donor will be able to receive income for as long as he or she is still alive. (If there are two spouses involved, income may be received for as long as both of the spouses are alive).

Also, the trust can name the charity to receive its proceeds at the death of the donor or donors. This means that the charity is considered to be the "remainder" beneficiary, because the charity will receive the "remainder" of the assets in the trust.

If the CRT is structured correctly, it shouldn't owe any capital gains taxes on the appreciation of assets that were inside of it. This can help the charity to receive a higher amount of assets when the time comes. The overall idea of a CRT is to reduce taxes for the donor (or donors) by first donating the assets into the trust, and then having the trust pay the beneficiary for the set period of time.

There are some variations of the charitable remainder trust. For instance, a Charitable Remainder Unitrust, or CRUT, is a trust agreement that splits benefits between an individual (or individuals) and a charity.

The donor transfers money or property, or both, into the trust in exchange for annual income payments. When the trust ends, the balance, or "remainder," is given to the charity as a gift from the donor.

There is also the Charitable Remainder Annuity Trust, or CRAT. This, too, is a type of planned giving vehicle that entails a donor placing a major gift of cash or property into a trust. The trust then pays a fixed amount of income each year to the donor or the donor's specified beneficiary. When the donor passes away, the remainder of the trust is then transferred to the charity.[4]

So, what is the key difference between a CRUT and a CRAT?

While a CRUT and a CRAT both appear to be similar - including in name - there is actually a difference between the two. With a Charitable Remainder Annuity Trust (CRAT), each year the trust will pay the donor a fixed percentage of the value of the donated assets at the time that those assets are placed into the trust.

In other words, the income stream will remain stable over the life of the trust. So, for instance, if a donor created a 20-year CRAT worth $100,000, then he or she would receive an annual income of $5,000 (assuming a minimum required annual payout of 5%).[5]

Alternatively, if you opt for a Charitable Remainder Unitrust, or CRUT, then you will also select a fixed annual payout ratio. (In this example, let's also say that the minimum is 5%). However, the actual dollar amount that you would receive each year can fluctuate, rather than remaining constant. That is because the assets that are held in a CRUT are re-valued at the beginning of each year. So, depending on the performance of those assets, you could earn more, or less, money each year.[6]

Leverage Your Estate with the Ultimate Asset Strategy - And Give Your Money Away Twice!

Providing for beneficiaries such as your loved ones and / or a favorite charity is a great strategy for ensuring that those you care about will benefit financially when you are gone. It is also a viable method of leaving a legacy.

But what's even better than giving your money away once?

How about giving it away twice!

Through use of a Charitable Remainder Annuity Trust (CRAT), you can do just exactly that. Let's take a look at an example that shows how this can be done. Cindy, a 70-year-old woman, had a 45-year-old daughter with a stable career.

Cindy was very involved in her church, and she wanted to leave her assets to the church so that it could continue its good works. Yet at the same time, Cindy also wanted to ensure that she left a nice inheritance for her daughter.

Unfortunately, like many investors and retirees, Cindy had been hit hard by the recession of 2008-2009. Yet, while many people in her situation had given up on charitable deductions since the recession and market crash, Cindy decided to rethink that decision and look at all of her options.

Ultimately, Cindy decided to transfer $250,000 to a Charitable Remainder Annuity Trust. In doing so, she named her church as the beneficiary. She also received an immediate tax deduction of more than $143,000 that could be spread over a six-year period (given her age and situation).

She was also able to pull back 8% of her donation each year - or $20,000 - which she subsequently paid into an Irrevocable Life Insurance Trust, or ILIT, in order to fund a $500,000 life insurance policy which named her daughter as the beneficiary.

In the process, Cindy was essentially able to give away her money twice, and upon her passing, her church will receive the $250,000 that was transferred to the trust. And her daughter will receive $500,000 tax-free from the insurance policy.

Had Cindy simply left her original $250,000 outright to her daughter, the biggest "winner" would have been Uncle Sam. That's because those $250,000 dollars would have been exposed to a tax bill in the neighborhood of $97,500 - which in turn would have only netted Cindy's daughter $152,500 - and in that scenario, Cindy's church would have received nothing.

But by going the route of the Charitable Remainder Annuity Trust, not only will Cindy's daughter net out $500,000 - which is roughly five times more than she would have by inheriting the taxable $250,000 - but the church will also benefit by gaining a quarter of a million dollars. On top of all that, Cindy was also able to take a write-off of approximately $143,000. This is truly an ultimate asset plan.

Unfortunately, many investors and retirees are not even aware that plans and strategies like this exist - proving that it is truly advantageous to work with an expert in the estate planning field so that you are aware of the various options that you may have available to you.

Charitable Lead Trust

Charitable lead trusts are actually designed to reduce beneficiaries' taxable income by first donating a portion of the trust's income to a charity. Then, after a set period of time, the remainder of the trust is then transferred to the beneficiary (or beneficiaries).[7]

Because of the way that it works, in some respects, a charitable lead trust can be considered to be the "opposite" of a charitable remainder trust. This is because with a charitable lead trust, assets are gifted into a charitable trust.

The trust then makes payments to the charity (or charities) of the donor's choosing. These payments can be for a certain amount of time, or for the remainder of the donor's lifetime. Likewise, the amount of the payments may either be a certain dollar amount, or they may be a certain percentage of the trust's overall value. At the end of the charitable lead trust's term, the principal that remains in the trust will then be distributed to the donor's family or alternatively to a trust for the benefit of his or her family.

Charitable lead trusts can be a good way to transfer wealth. One reason for this is because the value of the gift may be much more than its value for gift tax purposes. Also, the charitable lead trust could be designed so that the donor receives a charitable income tax deduction at the time that he or she creates the trust. (This would be based upon the "present value" of the income stream to the charity). Also, the charitable portion of the gift will reduce the amount of the donor's overall taxable estate value, in turn, reducing the amount of estate taxes that are due.

IRA Beneficiary Trust

IRA Beneficiary Trusts are a type of vehicle that can allow for your IRA distributions to be spread over one or more generations. This can be beneficial in a number of ways, starting with the fact that, because beneficiaries are not able to obtain all of the IRA funds at one time, it lessens the tax burden.

Throughout the past several years, the concept of the "stretch IRA" has become quite popular, as it provides various options for the beneficiaries. In this case, beneficiaries have the option of taking all the money at one time, and subsequently paying the taxes, or they can instead take the distributions over their lifetime, allowing the IRA to continue growing tax-deferred, and only paying taxes on the smaller annual distribution.

It is important to note, though, that in order for the beneficiaries to even have these options in the first place, the IRA must be set up properly. In addition, before stretching your IRA, you need to know that doing so can be a double-bladed sword.

For example, if the beneficiary only takes the Required Minimum Distribution (RMD), the IRA can continue to grow by a considerable amount, tax-deferred, over the longer time period. But on the other hand, nearly 90% of those who inherit money will squander it in less than 24 months.

The "minimum" distribution is also just the starting point, though. This is the amount that must be withdrawn - but the beneficiary can choose to withdraw more - and because of that, the money is oftentimes used up much more quickly than intended.

So, what can you do in order to avoid passing on your IRA, only to have it used up so quickly?

You can use an IRA Beneficiary Trust!

An IRA Beneficiary Trust can essentially provide the best of both worlds by allowing the benefit of stretching the account and let it continue growing tax-deferred, as well as the benefit of controlling the distributions to protect the account from things like lawsuits, creditors, and careless spending.

When an IRA Beneficiary Trust is created to be the recipient of the inherited IRA (or most other retirement accounts), it has special terms and conditions that empower the IRA Trust to maintain better control of the accounts. This is because the Trust is the owner of the inherited IRA account, and the Required Minimum Distributions are distributed to the Trust instead of directly to the beneficiary.

The Trustee must take out the Required Minimum Distribution each year. However, the Trust can specify when the beneficiary receives the distributions - which gives the trustee the ability to hold the funds in the Trust and reinvest then in other, non-tax deferred investments. This, in fact, is one of the most powerful benefits of the IRA Beneficiary Trust.

Yet another attractive benefit of the IRA Beneficiary Trust having the ability to hold the Required Minimum Distributions is that the funds can be held to protect them from frivolous spending by the beneficiaries, as well as the potential of losing funds due to lawsuits or divorce proceedings that involve the beneficiaries.

Trusts - Overview of Planning Benefits

	Avoidance of Probate	Wealth Transfer	Charitable Giving	Reduction of Estate Taxes
Revocable Living Trust	X	X		
Irrevocable Life Insurance Trust	X	X		X

Inter vivos Qualified Terminable Interest Property Trust		X		X
Grantor Retained Annuity Trust		X		X
Charitable Remainder Trust	X		X	X
Charitable Lead Trust	X	X	X	X
IRA Beneficiary Trust		X		

When working with trusts, it is always best to work with an estate planning attorney who has experience in setting up these types of documents, as most trusts will require very specific language.

Chapter 8 Sources

1. Life Insurance Premium Financing: Worth the Risk? By Jean Folger. February 3, 2017. Investopedia.

2. Ibid.

3. Grantor Retained Annuity Trust - GRAT. Investopedia.

4. Charitable Remainder Annuity Trust. Wikipedia. (https://en.wikipedia.org/wiki/Charitable_Remainder_Annuity_Trust)

5. CRAT versus CRUT: Choosing the Best Charitable Remainder Trust. Philanthro Media. (http://www.philanthromedia.org/archives/2004/10/crat_versus_crut_choosing_the.html)

6. Ibid.

7. Cypress Academy. Glossary.

Chapter 8 Quiz

Please complete this short quiz that covers information from Chapter 8. You can review the correct answers immediately after Question 5.

1. True or False: Asset protection is strictly for those who are wealthy.

2. _____ is the process of accumulating, preserving, and distributing assets in order to achieve your financial goals during your lifetime, and to provide for your heirs according to your wishes at death.

a. transferring

b. estate planning

c. allocating assets

d. None of the Above

3. Life insurance can be used in which of the following ways in the estate planning process?

a. Creating liquidity to pay estate settlement costs

b. Equalizing inheritances among family members

c. Making charitable donations

d. All of the Above

4. _____ involves taking out a third-party loan to pay for a life insurance policy's premiums.

a. 1035 exchange

b. premium financing

c. Both a and b

d. Neither a or b

5. True or False: Estate planning is not just a one-time event, but rather it is an ongoing process that is designed to accomplish accumulation, preservation, and distribution objectives, both during your life and following your death.

Chapter 8 Quiz Answers

1. False

2. b

3. d

4. b

5. True

Chapter 9:

What to Expect When You Create Your Plan

Who and What You Need to Construct Your Plan

"If you have some respect for people as they are, you can become more effective in helping them be better than they are."

John W. Gardner

The question of what you want your money to do can be much more difficult to answer than most people think. While most of us may dream of a nice relaxing future on the beach or the golf course and hope to help our kids and grandkids by leaving them something after we're gone, the reality is that the path of taking those thoughts to fruition must first be forged.

Consider Andy, a 60-year-old individual who currently has $300,000 in his IRA. Andy plans to retire soon and wants to make the most of his income, as well as to ensure that if his health starts to fail, he will have ample funds for those needs, too. Likewise, he would like to leave some money to his daughter when he is gone.

In Andy's present situation, should he pass away any time soon with his $300,000 IRA the way it is, his daughter will only end up with approximately $180,000 after Uncle Sam takes out its $120,000 tax.

However, if instead Andy were to pull out some of his IRA funds and put them into a specially designed plan that includes life insurance via an indexed universal life policy, he would be able to leave his daughter a $450,000 tax-free death benefit. And, should Andy require financial help due to a terminal illness or a stay in a nursing home, the policy includes "living benefits" that allow him to use a portion of the death benefit for these needs.

On top of all that, when Andy turns age 71, he could also receive a tax-free income benefit from the plan in the amount of roughly $22,000 per year. This could easily help him to supplement his income from Social Security over time.

How the Overall Estate Planning Process Works

Although the estate planning process may sound somewhat foreboding, the truth is that it can be quite simple - particularly if you are working with an expert in the field who walks you through the process each and every step of the way.

While all situations will differ, a basic estate plan typically includes the following:

- A will (which is also oftentimes referred to as a Last Will and Testament)
- Health care directive(s), such as an advanced directive, living will, and / or health care power of attorney, and
- A power of attorney that relates to the management of your assets.

Depending on the specific situation, an estate plan may also include a revocable living trust. This type of trust is sometimes referred to as a "will substitute," because it can take the place of a will in determining how assets pass at death. In addition, estate planning can include many other strategies, depending on the goals and objectives.

The estate planning process involves meeting with various advisors. (The members of your estate planning team are discussed in more detail in the next chapter). But before you discuss actual tools and strategies, it is first necessary to go over your goals - even if you are not yet 100% clear on them yet. Therefore, the focus of the initial discussion(s) should ideally be designed to achieve your goals and objectives in the most simply and efficient manner possible.

What Information is Needed from You

In order to create an estate plan that best meets your specific objectives, your attorney and financial advisor will need to know what your assets are, as well as how you wish to have them pass at your death.

You will also need to let your advisors know how your assets are owned or titled. For instance, do you own the property or asset solely, or rather with another person, such as your spouse or business partner. Likewise, some assets may be held or owned in an IRA or other type of retirement account. If you own any real estate, your advisors will need to know how exactly the ownership is stated on the deed.

With that in mind, you may need to do a bit of "homework" before you meet with your estate planning advisors. However, ensuring that all of the information is included is essential to ensuring that your plan is created properly.

Chapter 9 Quiz

In order to determine how much of the information from Chapter 9 you have retained, please complete the following five questions. The answers are located immediately following the chapter quiz.

1. Which of the following is / are typically included in a basic estate plan?

a. will

b. power of attorney

c. health care directive

d. All of the Above

2. True or False: Before you discuss actual estate planning tools and strategies, it is first necessary to go over your goals - even if you are not yet 100% clear on them yet.

3. True or False: If you own any real estate, your advisors will need to know how exactly the ownership is stated on the deed.

4. Another name for a will is a(n):

a. ILIT

b. Last Will and Testament

c. Both a and b

d. Neither a or b

5. True or False: It is never advisable for an estate plan to include a revocable living trust.

Chapter 9 Quiz Answers

1. d

2. True

3. True

4. b

5. False

Chapter 10:

Where to Go from Here

What a Difference a Day Makes

"Most people don't plan to fail, they fail to plan."

John L. Beckley

The many issues that surround the process of probate, creditors, and estate taxes, coupled with any potential legal proceedings and / or even con artists who may see an opportunity to gain from your hard-earned assets, can all prolong the time - and the expense - of settling your estate.

Because of these possible pitfalls, it is essential that you begin by getting the key pieces of your estate plan in place, and then moving forward from there. Doing so can best be accomplished by working with the right estate planning team.

Choosing the Right Estate Planning Team

Constructing your estate plan can be an extremely detailed process, and it is one that requires the careful eye of many different professionals in order to ensure that absolutely nothing has been overlooked.

Who are the most essential team members that will be needed?

There are several that are key for success. These include the following:

Attorney

First, you will need to choose an estate planning attorney. With so many legal issues that are related to estate planning, it is imperative that you obtain advice from a legal professional who specializes in these types of issues.

Financial / Insurance Advisor

Another essential member of your estate planning team is a financial advisor. He or she can help you in designing the proper asset allocation for your specific situation, goals, risk tolerance, and stage in life. They will also be able to monitor your investments throughout the changing market environment and make adjustments where and when necessary.

This individual may also be able to provide you with guidance into the estate plan in terms of how much and what type of insurance should be considered in order to meet the estate owner's estate liquidity needs, as well as the income needs of the survivors. In many ways, the financial advisor on your estate planning team is considered to be the "quarterback," as they will oftentimes coordinate everything into a complete planning package.

Tax Professional / CPA

You should also include a tax professional or CPA (Certified Public Accountant) on your team. This person or company can assist you in properly implementing tax strategies for taking advantage of available deductions and credits that you are eligible for. If you are an owner or partner in a business, this can be particularly beneficial.

Trust Company

A trust company can also be an important component in your estate plan. These entities are organized in order to perform the fiduciary duties of trusts. Trust companies are usually owned by banks or law firms and they may specialize in being a trustee for trusts, as well as for managing estates.

The trustee's duties can include managing and conserving estate assets, which can encompass jobs such as keeping the estate plan records, managing investments, paying medical expenses, and taking care of distributions of trust income and principal. The trust officer will help to set up and maintain trust arrangements according to the trust document that is prepared by your attorney.

Other Specialists

Depending on your specific needs and objectives - as well as the types of assets that you have - other professionals who have special expertise in areas such as real estate, art, or other collectibles may also be necessary members of your estate planning team.

Family Members

In addition to the involvement of the professionals, estate planning can also be a family affair that includes more than just the immediate family, as well as more than just the immediate family generations. This is why it is so important to ensure that the plan flows in all of the directions that it is supposed to.

What to Look for In a Financial Advisor

One of the key members of your estate planning team is the financial advisor. Today, there are many people who, after just a slight amount of training, can technically still call themselves a financial advisor.

But when you're considering decisions such as what will happen if you become disabled, and what will be done with your assets upon your passing, you definitely don't want to work with a "rookie." So, before you choose who you will work with, it is important that you gather some key information about this individual (or company).

Therefore, there are several important criteria that you should ideally look for in the financial advisor that you choose for your estate planning team. These include the following:

- Experience - As with any other important job, the experience of the person or team you choose is a key factor in how successful the end result will be.
- Education - Simply learning about a topic as versus performing all of the related duties well are two completely different things. Therefore, be sure that the financial advisor that you choose is someone who has in-depth education in the estate planning field - and that he or she continues to learn over time in order to keep up with new and different tools and strategies.
- Other Credentials / Professional Designations - There are several types of financial advisors. For instance, there are those who just simply are doing the job to earn a paycheck, and then there are others who truly dedicate themselves to the industry and their clients. In doing so, these individuals will typically earn various industry professional designations in order to learn more in-depth details about how they can better serve their customers.
- Background - When you turn your financial needs over to a financial planner, you will also want to be sure that he or she has a clean record. Therefore, be sure that you check their background in order to determine the individual's background. Online tools such as FINRA's Brokercheck (https://brokercheck.finra.org/) can be a beneficial resource for finding details regarding a financial advisor's employment history, certifications, licenses, and any violations.
- Area of Specialty - Because everyone's needs differ, it is not only important that you choose an experienced and educated financial planner, but also one who has a background in estate planning specifically. Today, there are many people who

call themselves financial advisors. But when it comes to the proper distribution of your hard-earned assets, be sure that the individual or the team you put your trust in is one that knows estate planning and all of its surrounding issues.

- Credibility - Working with a professional who has credibility is essential in terms of building a trusting relationship. Here, you will want the advisor to do what they say they are going to do. This is particularly the case as it pertains to the assets you've built up over a lifetime. In checking for credibility, be sure that you review any available customer testimonials. You may also want to directly contact some of the advisor's current and / or past clients in order to get a first-hand account their experiences.

Remember, your estate plan involves everything that you own - and more importantly, everyone that you love. Therefore, you can't leave anything to chance - and, there are no "do overs" if the plan doesn't work out as you had hoped.

Don't Just "Set It and Forget It"

An estate plan doesn't have to be complicated. It can be thorough enough to fit your needs, yet simple enough to focus on your key concerns. Estate plans can also start out small, and then grow with you as your needs change.

Once you have developed your estate plan, though, it isn't something that you just simply "set and forget." Rather, because life is a constant series of changes, your plan will need to change with you - and this starts with regularly reviewing it.

While there is no right or wrong time frame for these regular reviews, doing so at least once per year is generally recommended. However, you may need to do so more often if you have encountered any significant changes in your life, such as marriage or divorce, a birth or death in the family, the purchase or sale of a home or business, the receipt of an inheritance, and / or involvement in a lawsuit, just to name a few.

Planning Now Versus Planning Later

In its 7th Annual Industry Trends Survey, WealthCounsel and WealthManagement.com took a look at the business challenges of estate planning professionals, and in turn provided insight on what motivates people to engage in financial planning.

In this survey, it was found that the top three reasons people engage in planning are to:

1) Avoid probate (59%)

2) Minimize discord among beneficiaries (57%)

3) Protect children from mismanaging their inheritances (39%)

Yet, in spite of the survey results indicating that probate avoidance is foremost in the minds of those who engage in planning, the bad news is that the majority of Americans still don't plan because they lack the awareness as to why they should.[1]

But by not doing anything, you are essentially making the choice to throw caution to the wind and hope that all turns out ok for those you love and care about. But you are also likely well aware that "hope is not a strategy."

So, when it comes to the proper distribution of your estate - regardless of its amount - ask yourself if you're making any of these top estate planning mistakes:

- Letting your family go to probate court
- Believing that all living trust plans are the same
- Failing to address what will happen if you become disabled
- Not protecting your beneficiaries from themselves
- Not protecting your beneficiaries from third parties
- Thinking that your living trust covers your IRA and / or other retirement accounts
- Thinking that your living trust is enough
- Believing that the person(s) who you name to act as trustee will know what to do
- Not keeping up with any changes to your situation
- Procrastination[2]

If you've been putting off the creation (or completion) of your estate plan because you are "too busy," "too tired," or "not wealthy enough," or you believe that doing so will "cost too much," then know that you are putting the people you love the most in a highly unfavorable financial situation - one that could have been prevented with a plan.

What a Difference a Day Makes

Our lives, from beginning to end, are a series of individual days - and because of that, what we do with each and every day can make a difference. This is clearly exemplified in situations like the following story about one of our more recent clients. We'll call her Jane.

Jane was a 72-year-old woman who had worked as a tax preparer for more than four decades. Due in large part to the time that she spent preparing people's taxes, Jane rarely went out or did much of anything else during "tax time." Jane's 42-year-old son who had autism lived with her, although he worked every day through a special needs work-related program.

On April 12, 2017, I met with Jane, along with some friends from her church who had referred her to us. During our meeting, Jane revealed that she had roughly $1 million in total assets, however, she had no will in place, nor had she done any type of estate or wealth planning.

Given the time of year that we met (Jane's busy season for her business), I asked her, "Why now?" Her response was that, even though she had no notable health issues, the timing just felt right. So, we completed all of the necessary paperwork, and funded the Special Needs Trust that Jane had set up for her son.

But little did anyone know just how right Jane's timing for completing her estate planning would actually be.

April 12th was a Wednesday. On the following Monday, I received a phone call saying that Jane had passed away - and her passing occurred on the prior Thursday - just one day after completing her plan.

Thanks to the planning that Jane completed, the Special Needs Trust protected her son, and allowed him to live with people that he already knew and felt comfortable with - rather than becoming a ward of the state. Jane's plan also protected the assets that she had built up over time, so that they could be used by her son, who truly needed them, as versus having a bulk of her money going to Uncle Sam, as well as through the costly and time-consuming probate process.

Just one day literally made a substantial difference in this family's life. Have you put your wishes and your plan in place? If not, one day can make a world of difference by having the right documents in place at the right time...or not. And, when you work with the right professionals, the process can be much easier than you might think.

FRA Trust Advisors provides you with a three-step process to develop, fund, and execute your unique plan - all at one fixed cost. That way, there are no surprises. You know exactly what you can expect - and you'll have a completed plan that outlines a 360-

degree view of your entire financial picture (not just bits and pieces of it), and that provides for your wishes, all in just 21 days.

In a world that is filled with a long list of unknowns, you can still take control of protecting and preserving what you've worked for. Why not begin today!

Chapter 10 Sources

1. Top 10 Estate Planning Mistakes. FRA Trust.

2. Ibid.

Chapter 10 Quiz

The short quiz here on Chapter 10 will cover the key concepts that were covered here in this section. The correct answers are located immediately following the quiz.

1. Which of the following professionals should ideally be part of your estate planning team?

a. attorney

b. financial / insurance advisor

c. tax professional

d. All of the Above

2. True or False: In addition to the involvement of the professionals, estate planning can also be a family affair that includes more than just the immediate family, as well as more than just the immediate family generations.

3. Which of the following include some of the top estate planning mistakes that people make:

a. Procrastination

b. Letting their family go to probate court

c. Not protecting beneficiaries from themselves

d. All of the Above

4. In spite of survey results that indicate probate avoidance as being foremost in the minds of those who engage in estate planning, the majority of Americans actually still don't plan because _____.

a. they don't care what happens to their assets

b. they lack the awareness as to why they should

c. Both a and b

d. Neither a or b

5. True or False: Once you have completed your estate plan, the plan is set for life.

6. True or False: Your estate plan is completed and regularly updated so that those you love and care about won't have to endure the probate process or lose a substantial portion of your estate to unintended in-laws, outlaws, predators, or creditors?

Chapter 10 Quiz Answers

1. d

2. True

3. d

4. b

5. False

6. ?

Bonus Chapter:

How to Keep Your Future Income Out of Uncle's Sam's Pocket...and In Yours

Keeping More of Your Own Money Using STEP (Strategic Tax-free Evaluation Process)

What if I told you that, after all the years you've saved, invested, and planned for your retirement, you would have to hand over half – or possibly even much more – of your future income to Uncle Sam?

Not a pretty picture, is it?

But unfortunately, this scenario is much more probable than you might think. And because of that, most people will be shocked to learn that when you've finally reached the "finish line" in their working lives, the government will be the primary recipient of your investment income, pension benefits, and yes, possibly even your Social Security.

In fact, the better your investments have performed over the years, and the more income you generate, the more Uncle Sam likes it, because he – not you - will be the one reaping most of the reward.

Unfortunately, by the time you reach retirement, it's typically much too late to do anything to change this scenario. So, those who haven't planned ahead for this legalized highway robbery are usually stuck. This, in turn, can cause a significant impact in how you are able to spend the remainder of your time on this earth.

But it doesn't have to be that way.

There's a big financial storm on the horizon – one that could literally decimate the retirement income that you have available to spend. But there are ways that you can prepare for it – and in doing so, you can ensure that you are able to spend 100% of the future income you generate...regardless of what income tax rates are.

On top of that, you can also keep your hard-earned money safe in any economic environment, while at the same time, knowing that those you love will be financially secure – both now and long into the future.

Who Will Benefit More from Your Future Income – You or Uncle Sam?

Do you want to learn more about how you can keep more of your own money in your pocket – and out of Uncle Sam's – using our exclusive STEP (Strategic Tax-free Evaluation Process) strategy?

If so, I'd like to offer you my brand new book, Tax Free Retirement Income: Using the Exclusive STEP (Strategic Tax-free Evaluation Process) Strategy for Keeping Your Future Income Out of Uncle Sam's Pocket...and In Yours! as my FREE GIFT to you.

Just simply go to http://www.frafinancial.com/what-we-do/heres-to-the-good-life.php and let us know where you'd like us to send it.

If your savings and investments are racking up a big IOU to the IRS, it's time you took a STEP in a different direction. It's never too early or too late to get started!

To easily locate a trained STEP advisor, just simply go to: http://fratrust.com/next-step/. Or you can contact us directly by phone at 618-632-8558.

Resources

About FRA Trust

Since FRA Trust was first launched 30 years ago, we have grown to become a leading authority in all aspects of estate planning. We regularly deliver high-profile seminars across the United States, where we share our expertise in maximizing the value of your hard-earned assets to benefit you in your lifetime, and your family thereafter.

Our successful partnership with The Law Office and First National Bank in Sioux Falls allows us to provide estate planning, as well as legal and financial services, all in one convenient package.

For more information about FRA Trust, you can visit our website at:

www.FRATrust.com.

You can also contact us directly via phone or email at:

(800) 279-9785

marketing@fratrust.com

FRA Trust is conveniently located in O'Fallon, Illinois, at:

805 W. Highway 50

O'Fallon, IL 62269

What People Are Saying

"Informative. Great follow up completing exactly the documents we needed. The process builds trust and confidence. Most happy about our rep's complete knowledge and professionalism. Working with him made the whole process easy. Now that our estate is protected, a big weight is off our shoulders. Everything was completed as promised and we are completely satisfied."

- Allen & Phyllis Weiss

"The process was smooth; went very well. Clearly you guys were looking out for my best interests. I know I will have peace of mind and comfort. I have referred my family and friends to FRA Trust."

- Barbara Arnett

"We attended a seminar, and everyone seemed to be knowledgeable. Our rep was thorough and charming and made the process quite pleasant. The process was friendly, easy, and thorough. We were surprised at the ease and efficiency of the entire process. We now feel comfortable and secure knowing we have clear plans in place. We have referred several of our friends."

- Glen & Joyce McDaniel

"Your guys knew what they were talking about. They helped me see the necessity of getting this done and showed me the path to follow. Made me feel like I can trust them. Knowing that my estate is protected put my mind to rest. I tell everyone to get it done."

- Jean Bierbaum

"I found the seminar to be very informative, to the point that I wanted to learn more. The sincerity of the speaker was genuine and total honest. The advantages of a trust were clearly presented. I am reminded of the Greyhound commercials, 'Take the bus and leave the driving to us.' The experience was very comforting. I found the cost of setting

up a trust to be very reasonable and worthwhile. I feel very gratified and comforted knowing my estate is protected. If anyone is considering working with FRA Trust, be prepared for a very professional and rewarding experience."

- Kenneth G. Kenney Sr.

"I was referred by a friend and feel very satisfied working with FRA Trust."

- Lillian Dobelbower

"We attended a seminar and felt we were at the right place at the right time. The whole process was smooth. We have worried about getting a plan for a long time and are relieved to have our plan in place. FRA Trust people are very efficient and did a great job explaining things. They took the time to really help us understand the planning and process."

- Matthew & Sandra Kozyak

"The one-on-one process gave us a strong level of confidence in their services. We learned a lot. Knowing that our estate is protected put us at ease; we can relax."

- Neil & Averil Daniels

Disclaimer

This material is intended for education and training purposes only, and it is not intended to be, nor should it be construed as, an offer or solicitation for the purchase or sales of any specific securities, financial services, or other non-specified items. Securities products are sold by prospectuses containing more information about the product's fees, charges and limitations, and can only be offered by a qualified registered representative.

The material and concepts presented here are for informational purposes only and should not be construed as tax or legal advice. Please consult with your personal tax professional or legal advisor for further guidance on tax or legal matters.

All figures provided in this book are for illustrative purposes only and do not reflect an actual investment in any product, nor do they reflect the performance risks, expenses or charges associated with any actual investment. Past performance is not an indication of future performance. Actual results may vary substantially from the figures in the examples provided. All rates of return are hypothetical and are not a guarantee of future performance of any asset, including insurance or other financial products. Higher rates of return have been associated with higher volatility.

Examples of compound interest given in this book are strictly hypothetical and do not represent the past or future performance of any investment. Nor do they reflect any fees and charges associated with investments. It is unlikely that any one fixed rate of return would be sustained over time. Both the return and principal value of investments will fluctuate over time.

Guarantees provided in life insurance policies and annuity contracts are subject to the claims-paying ability of the issuing insurer.

Even though the interest credited to indexed annuity contracts or life insurance policies may be affected by an identified market index, these contracts or policies are not an investment in the stock market or the index and they do not participate in any stock or investment.

Generally, withdrawals from an annuity or a qualified retirement plan before age 59 1/2 are subject to a 10% federal tax penalty.

Generally, interest paid on municipal bonds is tax-free, but not all municipal bonds are exempt from federal and / or state income tax. Some bonds may be subject to capital gains tax at sale. Consult your tax advisor for more information.

A distribution from a Roth IRA generally is income tax-free if (a) it meets all the requirements for a qualified distribution [which include a 5-year waiting period and one of several additional requirements, one being that the distribution is made to a beneficiary on or after the death of the individual], or (b) it is a nonqualified distribution to the extent of after-tax contributions [basis].

For federal income tax purposes, life insurance death benefits generally pay income tax-free to beneficiaries pursuant to IRC Sec. 101(c)(1). In certain situations, however, life insurance death benefits may be partially or wholly taxable. Situations include, but are not limited to: the transfer of a life insurance policy for valuable consideration unless the transfer qualifies for an exception under IRC Sec. 101(a)(2) (i.e., the "transfer-for-value-rule"); arrangements that lack an insurable interest based on state law; and an employer-sponsored policy unless the policy qualifies for an exception under IRC Sec. 101(j).

Distributions such as loans and withdrawals from a life insurance policy can only be made if the policy has been in force long enough to accumulate sufficient value. Loans and withdrawals will reduce charges. If a policy lapses while a loan is outstanding, adverse tax consequences may result. Policy loans are generally not taxable when taken and cash withdrawals are not taxable until they exceed basis in the policy. However, if the policy is treated as a modified endowment contract (MEC) by IRS Sec. 7702A, withdrawals and loans may be taxable when taken to the extent of gain in the contract and may be subject to a 10% federal tax penalty if taken prior to age 59 1/2. Cash distributions associated with benefit reductions, including reductions caused by withdrawals during the first 15 years, may be taxable.

Glossary of Terms

401(k) - A form of private pension that provides tax advantages.

A/B Trust – A type of Revocable Living Trust that is for estate planning purposes, typically by married couples. This strategy uses two trusts – A and B – that are created when the first spouse passes away. The couple's assets are divided into two separate trusts when the first spouse dies, giving each spouse the ability to pass the maximum amount of assets allowed to avoid federal estate taxation.

Accountant - A professional who has been educated, trained, and authorized under applicable law to keep books or accounts, to perform financial audits, to design and control accounting systems, manage people's finances, and to give tax advice.

Administrator – An individual appointed by the court for the purpose of managing and distributing a probate estate if the decedent died without having a will.

ADR (American Depository Receipt) - A receipt issued by an American bank as a substitute for stock shares in a foreign-based corporation. ADRs are the most common method by which foreign companies secure American shareholders. Companies that offer ADRs maintain a stock listing in their domestic market in their domestic currency, while the ADRs are held in U.S. dollars and listed on a U.S. stock exchange, such as the New York Stock Exchange.

Advanced Healthcare Directive – A written document allowing an individual to provide specific instructions regarding medical treatment when they are deemed terminally ill or permanently unconscious. Also known as an advance directive.

Annual Exclusion – Each calendar year, individuals are allowed to gift a certain amount of property or assets to an unlimited number of others. In 2018, the amount of the annual gift exclusion is $15,000.

Annuity - 1) An obligation to pay a stated sum, usually monthly or annually, to a stated recipient. These payments terminate upon the death of the designated beneficiary. 2) A fixed sum of money payable periodically. 3) A right, often acquired under a life insurance contract, to receive fixed payments periodically for a specified duration. 4) A savings account with an insurance company or investment company, usually established for retirement income. Payments into the account accumulate tax-free, and the account is taxed only when the annuitant withdraws money in retirement.

Attorney - A professional who has been educated and trained to understand and practice the law and designated to transact business for another. Attorneys are usually specialists in specific areas such as probate attorneys, tax attorneys, etc.

Bank - A bank is a business that offers a place to keep money and uses it to make more money. Banks offer different services for keeping money.

Beneficiary - A person who is designated to benefit from an appointment, disposition, or assignment (as in a will, insurance policy, etc.); one designated to receive something as a result of a legal arrangement or instrument.

Bond - A debt of a corporation or government that it acknowledges and agrees to pay to the holder of the bond a certain fixed sum of money on a specified date and interest on that sum in the interim.

Budget - This term refers to a statement designed to coordinate resources and expenditures. It details what money is assigned or designated to, and what it is available for.

Capital Gains Elimination Trust - See Charitable Remainder Trust.

Capital Gains Tax - An income tax on the profits from the same of a capital asset.

Cash Flow - For purposes of this book, cash flow refers to the movement of money. Generating cash flow is producing and managing income to outweigh expenses. The "flow" in "cash flow" refers to the in and out motion of money - how it flows to and from one's pocketbook.

Certificate of Borrower Counseling - A document that certifies one's consultation with a Borrower Counselor that is required before obtaining a reverse mortgage.

Charitable Lead Trust - A trust in which a charity is named as the beneficiary for a period of time after which named individuals will succeed as the beneficiaries. These trusts are established to pass along assets that generate income to a charity. The benefit of these trusts is that they enable the grantor to still receive income while protecting the asset from taxes and probate.

Charitable Remainder Annuity Trust (CRAT) - A charitable remainder trust in which the named beneficiaries receive a fixed payment of not less than 5% of the fair market value of the original principal over the course of a specified period, after which the remaining principal passes to a charity.

Charitable Remainder Trust (CRT) - A trust in which the individuals named as beneficiaries retain the income from the trust for a designated period of time, usually the lifetime of the beneficiaries, after which the remainder passes to charity.

Charitable Remainder Unitrust - Charitable remainder trust in which the named beneficiaries receive payments of a fixed percentage, and not less than 5% of the value of the trust assets, as determined annually for a specified period, after which the remainder passes to charity.

Checking Account - A checking account is an account that lets an individual or a business owner write checks or use a debit card to pay bills and / or to make purchases.

Children's Trusts - These trusts are established when the beneficiary is a minor.

Closing - The final meeting between the parties to a transaction, at which the transaction is consummated; particularly in real estate, the final transaction between the buyer and the seller, whereby the conveyancing documents are concluded, and the money and the property are transferred.

Coinsurance - The amount that an insured is required to pay towards his or her medical costs. This amount varies with each medical insurance plan.

Compound Interest - Interest that is computed on the sum of a principal and accrued interest.

CPA - Certified Public Accountant.

Credit Bureau - A firm which collects and provides to creditors, employers, and insurers information on how consumers use credit, as well as other personal and financial data.

Credit File - All the information a consumer reporting agency has in its records on a particular consumer.

Credit Rating - A consumer's relative credit-worthiness as determined by a creditor, based on information obtained from a credit report, credit application, and interview.

Credit Report - A written, oral, or other communication from a credit bureau to a creditor, employer, or insurer concerning a consumer's credit history.

Credit Union - A nonprofit financial institution that is owned by people who have something in common. One must become a member of a credit union in order to keep money in it or to benefit from its other services.

Debt - A debt is an obligation to pay a particular person, company, bank, lender, or other entity.

Deduction - A deduction is typically used to describe money that is automatically taken from your paycheck; what is being subtracted from your income. Taxes, alimony or child support, insurance, union dues, and charitable are common deductions.

Deferred Annuity - An annuity that begins making payments on a specified date if the annuitant is alive at that time.

Deferred Compensation Plan - An employee's earnings that are taxed when received or distributed and not when earned, such as contributions to a qualified pension or profit-sharing plan.

Defined Benefit Plan - A plan that is established and maintained by an employer to provide systematically for the payment of determinable benefits to employees over a period of years after retirement, and usually for his or her lifetime. Retirement benefits under a defined benefit plan are measured by, and based upon, various factors, such as years of service rendered and compensation earned. The amount of benefits and the employer's contributions do not depend on the employer's profits. The employer bears the entire investment risk and it must cover any funding shortfall. Any plan that is not a defined contribution plan is a defined benefit plan.

Defined Contribution Plan - Under ERISA (the Employment Retirement Income Security Act), an employee retirement plan in which each employee has a separate account, funded by the employee's contributions and the employer's contributions (usually in a pre-set amount). The employee is entitled to receive the benefit generated by the individual account.

Deposit - A deposit is money that you add to a checking or savings account.

Devour Debt - Devour Debt is a debt elimination solution conceptualized by The Financial Gourmet. It is known as a "snowball" effect, where the smallest debt is paid off first, and then that payment amount is applied to the next largest debt, and so on.

Direct Deposit - With direct deposit, your paychecks or benefits checks are electronically transferred and directly deposited into your account. Some banks will waive monthly fees if direct deposit is used.

Discretionary Expenses - Unlike fixed expenses, these can vary from month to month, or even more frequently. You typically will have more control over discretionary expenses and are able to alter your monthly budget to accommodate them. You may also be able to curb your spending in a particular category by shopping or clipping coupons. You will find groceries, clothing, meals, entertainment, and personal goods in this expense category.

Dividend - A portion of a company's earnings or profits that are distributed pro rata to its shareholders, usually in the form of cash or additional shares.

Donee – A person who receives a gift.

Donor – A person who makes a gift.

Durable Power of Attorney (DPOA) - An instrument granting someone authority to act as agent or attorney-in-fact for the grantor that remains in effect during the grantor's incompetency. Such instruments commonly allow an agent to make healthcare decisions and financial decisions for someone who has become incompetent.

Dynasty Trust - Also referred to as a generation skipping trust, a dynasty trust allows you to transfer significant sums of cash, tax-free, to beneficiaries who are at least two generations younger than you (which is usually your grandchildren).

Emergency Fund - This is a separate stash of cash that you create and protect specifically for emergencies, such as car or home repairs, medical payments, or unexpected bills. It may also be used to pay a late fee on a credit card or an overdraft fee to a bank. Anything unbudgeted and unexpected can be covered using the emergency fund. A properly funded emergency fund will have three to six months of living expenses saved.

Estate - 1) All that a person or entity owns, including both real and personal property. 2) The collective assets and liabilities that one leaves after death.

Estate Plan – The written document setting out an estate owner's instructions for disposition and administration of his or her property at their death, incapacity, or total disability.

Estate Taxes - A tax imposed on property transferred by will or by intestate succession.

Executor - The person selected by the testator to complete the provisions of the testator's will.

Expenditure - See "Expense."

Expense - An expense is anything that causes a loss to your available cash flow. Utility bills, mortgage payments, groceries, bank fees, and tuition are all examples of possible expenses. Whatever causes you to reach for your wallet is considered to be an expense.

Family Trust - A family trust is also referred to as a credit shelter trust, or a bypass trust. For this trust variation, you write a will in which you bequeath a sum to the trust - up to the maximum figure for the estate tax exemption. The balance you will pass on to your spouse, tax-free. With a family trust, there is also an added bonus in that, once money is placed in it, no matter how much that money grows, it will always be free of estate tax.

Financial Planner - A financial planner is the architect of your entire strategy. This person understands the various components of a sound financial strategy and will work with you to create the best financial plan possible.

Fixed Expense - Fixed expenses are those expenses that do not vary much from month to month. You have little or no control over the amount of these expenses and therefore, they are fixed, or guaranteed. Examples of these may be your car payment, rent or mortgage.

Generation Skipping Trust (GST) - A trust that is established to transfer (usually principal) assets to a beneficiary more than one generation removed from the settlor. The transfer is often accomplished by giving some control or benefits (such as trust income) of the assets to a non-skip person, often a member of the generation between the settlor and skip person. This type of trust is subject to generation-skipping transfer tax.

Gift – A transfer of property without receiving some type of benefit in return. The person who makes the gift is not obligated in any way to make the transfer.

Grantor - See Trustor.

Heir - A person who, under the laws of intestacy, is entitled to receive an intestate decedent's property. Loosely, a person who inherits real or personal property, whether by will or by intestate succession.

Home Health Care Insurance - A type of coverage that is meant for long-term care as a person is either incapacitated or, with age, is in need of living assistance.

Immediate Annuity - A form of annuity paid for with a single premium that begins making payments back to the policy holder right away.

Income - It may seem fairly obvious, but income is more than the salary you earn. It also encompasses monies that are earned from investments, rental properties, annuities, side jobs, sale of personal property, alimony or child support, cash tips, or any other resources that increase the amount of money you use.

IRA (Individual Retirement Account) - A savings or brokerage account to which a person may contribute up to a specified amount of earned income each year. The contributions, along with any interest that is earned in the account, are not taxed until the money is withdrawn (with a Traditional IRA). Alternatively, the money may be withdrawn tax-free with a Roth IRA. The account holder could incur an additional 10% early withdrawal penalty from the IRS if he or she takes money out of the IRA account prior to turning age 59 1/2.

Irrevocable Life Insurance Trust (ILIT) – A trust whereby a life insurance policy is owned by the trust for the purpose of keeping the proceeds out of an individual's estate, thereby avoiding estate taxation on those proceeds.

Irrevocable Trust - A trust that cannot be terminated by the settlor once it is created.

Insurance Broker - This person can provide you with products that will fund your retirement, provide for your heirs, and protect your assets. A trained professional, an insurance broker is able to offer financial advice and provide insurance products, without an exclusive affiliation with a particular insurance company.

Interest - Interest is the extra money in your account that the bank or financial institution pays you for keeping your money.

Inter Vivos Trust - A trust that is created by you and takes effect during your lifetime.

Intestate - Of or relating to a person who has died without a valid will.

Joint Ownership – The situation where two or more people own the same piece of property together. There are a number of ways property can be jointly owned, including as joint tenants, tenants in common, tenants by the entirety, or other legally defined relationships.

Joint Tenancy – When two or more people take title to the same property and simultaneously each owns 100% of the property, or has full rights to the property. At the death of one joint tenant, his or her share will immediately transfer to the ownership of the survivor(s).

Keogh Plan - A tax-deferred retirement program that is available to those who are self-employed.

Legatee - One who has been named in a will to take personal property; one who has received a legacy or bequest.

Life Estate – An individual has the benefits of a property during their lifetime, however, they do not own the property and therefore when they die, the property is thus not included in their estate.

Life Insurance - A contract between an insurance policy holder and an insurer, where the insurer promises to pay a designated beneficiary a sum of money (the benefits) upon the death of the insured person.

Living Trust – A type of revocable trust that is used in estate planning in order to avoid probate, help in situations of incompetency, and allow smooth management of assets after the death of the grantor or person who established the trust. The trust can be effective in eliminating or reducing estate taxes for married couples.

Living Will – A document that defines your "right to die." This document typically states that you do not want to have your life artificially prolonged by modern medical technologies.

Long-Term Care Insurance - An insurance product sold in the United States, United Kingdom, and Canada, which helps provide for the cost of long-term care beyond a pre-determined period. Long-term care insurance covers care that is generally not covered by health insurance, Medicare, or Medicaid.

Long-Term Care Policy - A policy option that will make payments towards long-term care expenses. Most long-term care policies today will pay for care that is received in a facility and / or at the recipient's home.

Marital Deduction – Married couples are allowed to pass to their spouse an unlimited amount of assets upon the first spouse's death without being subject to estate taxation.

Medicaid - A federal and state government health care program that is designed to help those in financial need.

Medicare - A federal health care insurance program that provides health insurance to the elderly and the disabled.

Money Market Fund - A mutual fund that invests in low-risk government securities and short-term notes.

Mutual Fund - A form of investment in which your contribution is "pooled" with the contributions of others. Mutual funds are managed by an institution, and you do not have contact with other investors.

Multigenerational IRA - Also referred to as an Extended IRA or Stretch IRA. A term used to refer to an IRA that allows the first-generation beneficiary to designate a successor beneficiary (or successor beneficiaries) of an inherited IRA, and for the IRA to be passed on to a succession of beneficiaries over the life expectancy of the first-generation beneficiary.

National Debt - The amount of money the United States government owes to other entities.

Net Taxable Estate – The net taxable estate or net value is the total or gross value of the estate less liabilities, expenses, and other deductions that are allowed by the tax laws. The result is the value of the estate upon which the federal estate tax will be levied.

Periodic Expense - A periodic expense is one that is not paid routinely, as in monthly. These expenses may be paid quarterly or annually. Examples may be property taxes or vehicle registration. It may be a fixed expense or a discretionary expense, but it is one that requires careful planning to be paid.

Personal Property – Property other than real estate (land and permanent structures on the land). Cars, furniture, securities, bank accounts, and animals are all examples of personal property.

Portfolio - A complete list of all of your investments.

Power of Attorney – Legal document that grants another individual the authority to manage the financial affairs of another. This document becomes invalid when the individual dies or becomes incompetent, unless it is deemed as a durable power of attorney.

Private Pension - A pension plan that is established either through your employer or on your own. These plans may or may not qualify for tax advantages. Private pensions differ from public pensions, which are provided to government employees.

Probate - The process whereby the probate courts divide the estate of a deceased person among the creditors and heirs.

Probate Attorney - A legal professional who specializes in probate law and the processes of assigning the proceeds of an estate.

Probate Court - The court with the power to declare wills valid or invalid, to oversee the administration of estates, and in some states to appoint guardians and approve the adoption of minors.

Pension - A fixed sum that is paid regularly to a person or dependents following retirement by a private employer or the U.S. Government.

Public Pension - A pension plan that is provided to various government employees.

Qualified Retirement Plan - A retirement plan established through your employer that meets the requirements for tax breaks.

Reverse Mortgage - A mortgage in which the lender disburses money over a long period of time to provide regular income to the (usually elderly) borrower, and in which the loan is repaid in a lump sum when the borrower dies or when the property is sold. A form of income creation that takes advantage of the capital that is already invested in a home.

Revocable Trust – A trust which can be amended or revoked by the person(s) who established the trust.

Roth IRA - A Roth IRA is an individual retirement account that offers a valuable tax break - tax-free income in retirement. Because of that, the money that goes into a Roth IRA is after-tax money.

Savings Account - A savings account is an account that earns interest. You can open a savings account with just a few dollars, but you may also need to pay a monthly or annual fee if your balance falls below a certain dollar amount.

Settlor – A person who establishes a trust. The term settler is used interchangeably with the terms "trustor" and "grantor."

Social Security - A federal government program to which all employees and employers contribute that is designed to provide some old-age and survivors' benefits.

Taxable Estate – The portion of an estate that is subject to federal estate taxes or state death taxes. Technically, all of an estate is subject to federal estate taxes, but because of the unified credit, only estates with a value over the exemption equivalent amount actually have to pay any estate taxes.

Tenants by the Entirety – Similar to owning property via joint tenancy. With this method, the joint tenancy is allowed to be used by anyone, regardless of whether or not they are a married couple.

Tenants in Common – Method of owning property whereby two or more owners "share" ownership in an asset or a property. Each owner is able to own different percentages of the property – they do not all have to own an equal share.

Testamentary Trust - A trust that is created through a will and that becomes effective at the testator's death.

Testator - A person who, at death, leaves a valid will.

Three-Legged Stool - This is a term that is oftentimes used to describe how retirement used to be viewed as a three-pronged approach, meaning: Social Security, employer-funded pension programs, and personal savings.

Transfers of Assets or Spend-down - This practice is prohibited for purposes of establishing Medicaid eligibility. Applies when assets are transferred, sold, or gifted for less than they are actually worth by individuals in long-term care facilities or who are receiving home and community-based waiver services, by their spouses, or by someone else who is acting on their behalf.

Trust - A legal agreement in which the trustor places assets in the possession of a trustee for the benefit of the trust beneficiary.

Trustee - The person, professional, or institution who manages the assets of the trust under the terms of the trust declaration.

Trustor - A person who intentionally creates a trust. Also known as a settlor or grantor.

Unified Credit – A tax credit is given to each person by the IRS to be used during his or her life or after his or her death. The tax credit equals the amount of tax (gift or estate) which is assessed on the exemption equivalent value of property. It is considered to be the "unified" credit because it applies to both gift taxes and estate taxes and results from the IRA's effort to unify these two taxes or make them consistent.

Unlimited Marital Deduction – The tax law that allows a person to give an unlimited value of property as a gift, or leave an estate of unlimited value to his or her spouse without a gift or estate tax being assessed.

Will – A legal document that states the intentions of a deceased person concerning the distribution of his or her assets and property, as well as the management of his or her affairs following their death. State law typically dictates the legality of a will.

Made in the USA
Monee, IL
26 May 2024

58664285R00085